EDWARD ALBEE

Modern Critical Views

Henry Adams
Edward Albee
A. R. Ammons
Matthew Arnold
John Ashbery
W. H. Auden
Jane Austen
James Baldwin
Charles Baudelaire
Samuel Beckett
Saul Bellow
The Bible
Elizabeth Bishop
William Blake
Jorge Luis Borges
Elizabeth Bowen
Bertolt Brecht
The Brontës
Robert Browning
Anthony Burgess
George Gordon, Lord
   Byron
Thomas Carlyle
Lewis Carroll
Willa Cather
Cervantes
Geoffrey Chaucer
Kate Chopin
Samuel Taylor Coleridge
Joseph Conrad
Contemporary Poets
Hart Crane
Stephen Crane
Dante
Charles Dickens
Emily Dickinson
John Donne & the Seven-
   teenth-Century Meta-
   physical Poets
Elizabethan Dramatists
Theodore Dreiser
John Dryden
George Eliot
T. S. Eliot
Ralph Ellison
Ralph Waldo Emerson
William Faulkner
Henry Fielding
F. Scott Fitzgerald
Gustave Flaubert
E. M. Forster
Sigmund Freud
Robert Frost

Robert Graves
Graham Greene
Thomas Hardy
Nathaniel Hawthorne
William Hazlitt
Seamus Heaney
Ernest Hemingway
Geoffrey Hill
Friedrich Hölderlin
Homer
Gerard Manley Hopkins
William Dean Howells
Zora Neale Hurston
Henry James
Samuel Johnson and
   James Boswell
Ben Jonson
James Joyce
Franz Kafka
John Keats
Rudyard Kipling
D. H. Lawrence
John Le Carré
Ursula K. Le Guin
Doris Lessing
Sinclair Lewis
Robert Lowell
Norman Mailer
Bernard Malamud
Thomas Mann
Christopher Marlowe
Carson McCullers
Herman Melville
James Merrill
Arthur Miller
John Milton
Eugenio Montale
Marianne Moore
Iris Murdoch
Vladimir Nabokov
Joyce Carol Oates
Sean O'Casey
Flannery O'Connor
Eugene O'Neill
George Orwell
Cynthia Ozick
Walter Pater
Walker Percy
Harold Pinter
Plato
Edgar Allan Poe
Poets of Sensibility & the
   Sublime

Alexander Pope
Katherine Ann Porter
Ezra Pound
Pre-Raphaelite Poets
Marcel Proust
Thomas Pynchon
Arthur Rimbaud
Theodore Roethke
Philip Roth
John Ruskin
J. D. Salinger
Gershom Scholem
William Shakespeare
   (3 vols.)
   Histories & Poems
   Comedies
   Tragedies
George Bernard Shaw
Mary Wollstonecraft
   Shelley
Percy Bysshe Shelley
Edmund Spenser
Gertrude Stein
John Steinbeck
Laurence Sterne
Wallace Stevens
Tom Stoppard
Jonathan Swift
Alfred, Lord Tennyson
William Makepeace
   Thackeray
Henry David Thoreau
Leo Tolstoi
Anthony Trollope
Mark Twain
John Updike
Gore Vidal
Virgil
Robert Penn Warren
Evelyn Waugh
Eudora Welty
Nathanael West
Edith Wharton
Walt Whitman
Oscar Wilde
Tennessee Williams
William Carlos Williams
Thomas Wolfe
Virginia Woolf
William Wordsworth
Richard Wright
William Butler Yeats

These and other titles in preparation

Modern Critical Views

EDWARD ALBEE

Edited and with an introduction by

Harold Bloom
Sterling Professor of the Humanities
Yale University

CHELSEA HOUSE PUBLISHERS ◇ 1987
New York ◇ New Haven ◇ Philadelphia

© 1987 by Chelsea House Publishers, a division of Chelsea
House Educational Communications, Inc.,
    95 Madison Avenue, New York, NY 10016
    345 Whitney Avenue, New Haven, CT 06511
    5014 West Chester Pike, Edgemont, PA 19028

Introduction © 1987 by Harold Bloom

Printed and bound in the United States of America

∞ The paper used in this publication meets the minimum
requirements of the American National Standard for
Permanence of Paper for Printed Library Materials,
Z39.48-1984.

Library of Congress Cataloging-in-Publication Data
Edward Albee.
    (Modern critical views)
    Bibliography: p.
    Includes index.
    Contents: Albee and the absurd/Brian Way—Edward
Albee/Gerald Weales—Albee's Gothic/Paul Witherington—
[etc.]
    1. Albee, Edward, 1928–   —Criticism and
interpretation.   [1. Albee, Edward, 1928–   —Criticism and interpretation.   2. American literature—History
and criticism]   I. Bloom, Harold.   II. Series.
PS3551.L25Z65   1987   812'.54   86-29943
ISBN 0-87754-707-6 (alk. paper)

Contents

Editor's Note

This book gathers together the best criticism that has been devoted to the plays of Edward Albee. The critical essays are arranged here in the chronological order of their original publication. I am grateful to Henry Finder for his erudition and judgment in helping me to edit this volume.

My introduction first considers the relation of Albee's work to Tennessee Williams's dramas and then seeks to estimate Albee's achievement in *The Zoo Story* and in *Who's Afraid of Virginia Woolf?*. Brian Way begins the chronological sequence with an analysis of *The American Dream* and *The Zoo Story* that compares Albee to such dramatists of the absurd as Beckett and Pinter and finds him to be far more deeply contaminated by a theater of naturalistic reality than they are. In an overview of Albee's career, Gerald Weales finds a consistent lack in what he calls the dramatic image fully realized on stage.

Paul Witherington, examining *Tiny Alice* as an instance of Gothic drama, works back through the sequence of Albee's plays to find similar instances of the Gothic mode. Reviewing *All Over*, Ronald Hayman sees in it one of the more hopeful instances of the conflict between Beckett and Broadway in Albee. In remarks upon *Box* and *Quotations from Chairman Mao*, Anthony Hopkins uncovers Albee's continuing obsession with American moral decay.

Tiny Alice is studied by Mary Castiglie Anderson as a Jungian drama that depicts the archetypes of the collective unconscious. Julian Wasserman, examining the language of Albee's work, sees it as imitating the quest of the linguist, which is to turn fact into truth. *Seascape*, according to Liam O. Purdon, is a romance that aspires to the development of a higher state of consciousness, and so is essentially optimistic.

Considering *The Lady from Dubuque*, Thomas P. Adler relates the play to Pirandello's similar treatments of the problem of knowing. C. W. E. Bigsby, centering upon *Who's Afraid of Virginia Woolf?*, reads the drama as a representation of the destruction of imagination by infantile fears. In a final essay, Matthew C. Roudané returns us to Pirandello's influence upon Albee in *The Man Who Had Three Arms*.

vii

Introduction

Edward Albee is the crucial American dramatist of his generation, standing as the decisive link between our principal older dramatists—Eugene O'Neill, Thornton Wilder, Tennessee Williams, Arthur Miller—and the best of the younger ones—Sam Shepard and David Mamet, among others. Though Albee's best work came at his beginnings, with *The Zoo Story*, *The American Dream*, and *Who's Afraid of Virginia Woolf?*, he is hardly, at fifty-eight, to be counted out. A way into his aesthetic dilemmas is provided by the one-scene play *Fam and Yam: An Imaginary Interview*, written and staged in 1960, the year of *The American Dream*. Fam, a Famous American Playwright, is called upon by Yam, a Young American Playwright, in what is clearly an encounter between a precursor, say Tennessee Williams, and a rising latecomer, say Edward Albee. Yam is the author of an off-Broadway play, *Dilemma, Dereliction and Death*, which sounds rather like a three-word summary of *The Zoo Story*. The outer, single joke of *Fam and Yam* is that the Famous American Playwright is tricked into an interview by the Young American Playwright, but the meaning of the skit, uneasily riding its surface, is a dramatic version of the anxiety of influence (to coin a phrase).

Haunted by Williams, Albee was compelled to swerve from the master into a lyrical drama even more vehemently phantasmagoric than *The Glass Menagerie* and even more incongruously fusing realism and visionary illusion than *A Streetcar Named Desire*. The force of Albee's initial swerve was undeniable; *The Zoo Story*, his first play (1958), still seems to me his best, and his most ambitious and famous drama remains *Who's Afraid of Virginia Woolf?* (1961–62). After *Tiny Alice* (1964), Albee's inspiration was pretty well spent, and more than twenty years later, he still matters for his intense flowering between the ages of thirty and thirty-six. The shadow of Williams, once held off by topological cunning and by rhetorical gusto, lengthened throughout all of Albee's plays of the 1970s. Hart Crane, Williams's prime precursor, can give the motto for Albee's relationship to Williams:

1

Have you not heard, have you not seen that corps
Of shadows in the tower, whose shoulders sway
Antiphonal carillons launched before
The stars are caught and hived in the sun's ray?

II

   Any grouping of the strongest American dramas would have to include
The Iceman Cometh and *Long Day's Journey into Night*, *Death of a Salesman* and
The Skin of Our Teeth, *A Streetcar Named Desire* and *The Zoo Story*. A play in
one scene, *The Zoo Story* remains a marvel of economy. The highest tribute
one can make to it is to say that it is worthy of its stage history. I saw it
during its first American production, in early 1960, when it shared a double
bill, off Broadway, with Beckett's extraordinary *Krapp's Last Tape*. The Gnos-
tic sublimity of Beckett's most powerful stage work (except for *Endgame*)
ought to have destroyed any companion of the evening, but Albee's mordant
lyrical encounter not only survived but took on an added lustre through the
association.

   I am not certain that *The Zoo Story* has any peers among the shorter
works of O'Neill, Wilder, and Williams. Albee's first play, after more than
a quarter-century, remains a shot out of Hell, worthy of such authentic
American visions of the abyss as West's *Miss Lonelyhearts* and Pynchon's *The
Crying of Lot 49*. Both Peter and Jerry are triumphs of representation; re-
reading the play is to renew one's surprise as to how vivid they both remain,
particularly Peter, so apparently pale and stale compared to the demonic
and indeed psychotic Jerry. Yet Peter retains an intense aesthetic dignity,
without which the play could neither be staged nor read. Essentially Peter
represents us, the audience, rather in the way that Horatio represents us.
Jerry is a New York City Hamlet—mad in all directions, even when the
wind blows from the south, and manifestly he is a kind of Christ also. Peter
is therefore Peter the denier as well as Horatio, the institutional rock upon
which the church of the commonplace must be built.

   The psychosexual relationship between Jerry and Peter necessarily is
the center of *The Zoo Story*, since the zoo story is, as Jerry desperately
observes, that indeed we all are animals, dying animals, in Yeats's phrase:

JERRY: Now I'll let you in on what happened at the zoo; but
         first, I should tell you why I went to the zoo. I went to
         the zoo to find out more about the way people exist with
         animals, and the way animals exist with each other, and

with people too. It probably wasn't a fair test, what with
everyone separated by bars from everyone else, the
animals for the most part from each other, and always the
people from the animals. But, if it's a zoo, that's the way
it is. (*He pokes* PETER *on the arm*) Move over.

PETER (*Friendly*): I'm sorry, haven't you enough room? (*He shifts
a little*)

JERRY (*Smiling slightly*): Well, all the animals are there, and all
the people are there, and it's Sunday and all the children
are there. (*He pokes* PETER *again*) Move over.

PETER (*Patiently, still friendly*): All right.
(*He moves some more, and* JERRY *has all the room he might need*)

JERRY: And it's a hot day, so all the stench is there, too, and all
the balloon sellers, and all the ice cream sellers, and all the
seals are barking, and all the birds are screaming. (*Pokes*
PETER *harder*) Move over!

PETER (*Beginning to be annoyed*): Look here, you have more than
enough room! (*But he moves more, and is now fairly cramped
at one end of the bench*)

JERRY: And I am there, and it's feeding time at the lions' house,
and the lion keeper comes into the lion cage, one of the
lion cages, to feed one of the lions. (*Punches* PETER *on the
arm, hard*) MOVE OVER!

PETER (*Very annoyed*): I can't move over any more, and stop
hitting me. What's the matter with you?

Jerry begins with a cruel parody of Walt Whitman's *Song of Myself*,
section 32, where the American bard idealizes the supposed difference between animals and ourselves:

> I think I could turn and live with animals,
> > they are so placid and self-contain'd,
> I stand and look at them long and long.

> They do not sweat and whine about their
> > condition,
> They do not lie awake in the dark and
> > weep for their sins.
> They do not make me sick discussing
> > their duty to God.

The mounting hysteria of Jerry demystifies Whitman, and is answered by a rising terror in Peter. Only the catastrophic impaling of Jerry allows Jerry's zoo story to be finished:

> PETER (*Breaks away, enraged*): It's a matter of genetics, not manhood, you . . . you monster.
> (*He darts down, picks up the knife and backs off a little; he is breathing heavily*)
> I'll give you one last chance; get out of here and leave me alone!
> (*He holds the knife with a firm arm, but far in front of him, not to attack, but to defend*)
>
> JERRY (*Sighs heavily*): So be it!
> (*With a rush he charges* PETER *and impales himself on the knife. Tableau: For just a moment, complete silence,* JERRY *impaled on the knife at the end of* PETER's *still firm arm. Then* PETER *screams, pulls away, leaving the knife in* JERRY. JERRY *is motionless, on point. Then he, too, screams, and it must be the sound of an infuriated and fatally wounded animal. With the knife in him, he stumbles back to the bench that* PETER *had vacated. He crumbles there, sitting, facing* PETER, *his eyes wide in agony, his mouth open*)
>
> PETER (*Whispering*): Oh my God, oh my God, oh my God.
> (*He repeats these words many times, very rapidly*)
>
> JERRY (JERRY *is dying; but now his expression seems to change. His features relax, and while his voice varies, sometimes wrenched with pain, for the most part he seems removed from his dying. He smiles*): Thank you, Peter. I mean that, now; thank you very much.
> (PETER's *mouth drops open. He cannot move; he is transfixed*)
> Oh, Peter, I was so afraid I'd drive you away. (*He laughs as best he can*) You don't know how afraid I was you'd go away and leave me. And now I'll tell you what happened at the zoo. I think . . . I think this is what happened at the zoo . . . I think. I think that while I was at the zoo I decided that I would walk north . . . northerly, rather . . . until I found you . . . or somebody . . . and I decided that I would talk to you . . . I would tell you things . . . and things that I would tell you would . . . Well, here we are. You see? Here we *are*. But . . . I don't

know . . . could I have planned all this? No . . . no, I
couldn't have. But I think I did. And now I've told you
what you wanted to know, haven't I? And now you know
all about what happened at the zoo. And now you know
what you'll see in your TV, and the face I told you about
. . . you remember . . . the face I told you about . . . my
face, the face you see right now. Peter . . . Peter? . . .
Peter . . . thank you. I came unto you (*He laughs, so
faintly*) and you have comforted me. Dear Peter.

PETER (*Almost fainting*): Oh my God!

JERRY: You'd better go now. Somebody might come by, and
you don't want to be here when anyone comes.

PETER (*Does not move, but begins to weep*): Oh my God, oh my
God.

JERRY (*Most faintly, now; he is very near death*): You won't be
coming back here any more, Peter; you've been
dispossessed. You've lost your bench, but you've defended
your honor. And Peter, I'll tell you something now;
you're not really a vegetable; it's all right, you're an
animal. You're an animal, too. But you'd better hurry
now, Peter. Hurry, you'd better go . . . see?
(*JERRY takes a handkerchief and with great effort and pain wipes
the knife handle clean of fingerprints*)
Hurry away, Peter.
(*PETER begins to stagger away*)
Wait . . . wait, Peter. Take your book . . . book. Right
here . . . beside me . . . on your bench . . . my bench,
rather. Come . . . take your book.
(*PETER starts for the book, but retreats*)
Hurry . . . Peter.
(*PETER rushes to the bench, grabs the book, retreats*)
Very good, Peter . . . very good. Now . . . hurry away.
(*PETER hesitates for a moment, then flees, stage-left*)
Hurry away. . . . (*His eyes are closed now*) Hurry away,
your parakeets are making the dinner . . . the cats . . . are
setting the table.

PETER (*Off stage*):
(*A pitiful howl*)
OH MY GOD!

JERRY (*His eyes still closed, he shakes his head and speaks; a

combination of scornful mimicry and supplication): Oh . . . my
. . . God.
(*He is dead*)

CURTAIN

Screaming with the fury of a fatally wounded animal, Jerry begins his
final moments, attempting to tell Peter and the audience just what happened
at the zoo, yet failing to do so, because he himself does not quite know what
happened to him there. Though he speaks the language of annunciation,
reversed ("I came unto you and you have comforted me"), his only revelation
to Peter, and to us, is that: "it's all right, you're an animal. You're an animal,
too." The battle for the park bench, a territorial imperative, has exposed to
Peter, our Horatio and surrogate, that we are all animals also. Jerry's mission
ends with that message, and so he is happy to die. What is superb and
dreadful about Albee's great short drama is that its apocalyptic burden is
both Freudian and Christian. Through Peter, we are taught again that we
are all bisexual, though many if not most of us repress that psychic com-
ponent. Yet we are taught also that, without the transcendental and extraordinary, we are animals indeed. The zoo story is that, without grace or a
selfless love, we impale or are impaled.

III

The fame of *Who's Afraid of Virginia Woolf?*, primarily because of the
popular if flawed Mike Nichols film, with Elizabeth Taylor and Richard
Burton, tends to obscure its close resemblance to *The Zoo Story*, since again
we have a drama of impaling, of love gone rancid because of a metaphysical
lack. That is Albee's characteristic and obsessive concern, marked always
by its heritage, which is a similar sense of the irreconcilability of love and
the means of love that dominates the plays of Tennessee Williams. Unfortunately, *Who's Afraid of Virginia Woolf?* is a kind of blowup of *The Zoo Story*
and aesthetically is inferior to it, whether in the study or on the stage. Martha
and George paradoxically are a less memorable couple than Jerry and Peter,
perhaps because both of them, like Peter, are surrogates for the audience.
Neither of them has Jerry's Hamlet-like quality of being ourselves, yet
considerably beyond us. Instead, both Martha and George are Horatios,
who survive only to endure the endless repetition of drawing their breaths,
in this harsh world, in order to go on telling our story.

The undenied power as representation of Albee's *Virginia Woolf* is that
it has become as much our contemporary version of middle-class marriage

as O'Neill's *Long Day's Journey into Night* has established itself as our modern version of the American family. Yet that raises the issue of social mythology rather than of the mimesis of human reality. Albee, like O'Neill and like his own precursor, Williams, is open to the accusation that he has become more a caricaturist than a dramatist. George and Martha are cartoon figures; they cannot surprise us any more than they can surprise one another. They are shrewd imitations of a conventional foreshortening of reality, psychic and societal, a foreshortening that, alas, many of us live. But they do not compel aspects of reality, that we could not see without them, to appear, and they are incapable of change. In some sense, they cannot even listen to themselves, let alone one another. If you cannot hear yourself speak, then you cannot change by pondering what you yourself have said, which is one of the great implicit Shakespearean lessons. *The Zoo Story* had learned that lesson, but *Who's Afraid of Virginia Woolf?* has forgotten it.

One way of observing Albee's decline in power of representation between *The Zoo Story* and *Virginia Woolf* is to contrast our first and last visions of George and Martha, and then juxtapose that contrast to the shocking difference between our first and last visions of Jerry and Peter, the protagonists of *The Zoo Story*. Jerry ends as a pragmatic suicide, and Peter as an involuntary murderer, or manslaughterer, yet their more profound change is from being total strangers to being something like fatal lovers. But, because they are caricatures, can George and Martha change at all?

GEORGE: I'm tired, dear . . . it's late . . . and besides. . . .

MARTHA: I don't know what you're so tired about . . . you haven't *done* anything all day; you didn't have any classes, or anything.

GEORGE: Well, I'm tired. . . . If your father didn't set up these goddamn Saturday night orgies all the time. . . .

MARTHA: Well, that's too bad about you, George.

GEORGE (*Grumbling*): Well, that's how it is, anyway.

MARTHA: You didn't *do* anything; you never *do* anything; you never *mix*. You just sit around and *talk*.

GEORGE: What do you want me to do? Do you want me to act like you? Do you want me to go around all night *braying* at everybody, the way you do?

MARTHA (*Braying*): I DON'T BRAY!

GEORGE (*Softly*): All right . . . you don't bray.

MARTHA (*Hurt*): I do not *bray*.

GEORGE: All right. I said you didn't bray.

MARTHA (*Pause*): I'm cold.

GEORGE: It's late.

MARTHA: Yes

GEORGE (*Long silence*): It will be better.

MARTHA (*Long silence*): I don't . . . know.

GEORGE: It will be . . . maybe.

MARTHA: I'm . . . not . . . sure.

GEORGE: No.

MARTHA: Just . . . us?

GEORGE: Yes.

MARTHA: I don't suppose, maybe, we could. . . .

GEORGE: No, Martha.

MARTHA: Yes. No.

GEORGE: Are you all right?

MARTHA: Yes. No.

GEORGE (*Puts his hand gently on her shoulder; she puts her head back and he sings to her, very softly*): Who's afraid of
Virginia Woolf
Virginia Woolf
Virginia Woolf,

MARTHA: I . . . am . . . George.

GEORGE: Who's afraid of Virginia Woolf.

MARTHA: I . . . am . . . George. . . . I . . . am.

(GEORGE *nods, slowly*)

(*Silence; tableau*)

CURTAIN

George talks, ineffectually; Martha brays, ineffectually; that is their initial reality, when we come upon them. Martha barely talks, or is silent; George is almost equally monosyllabic, when we leave them. A silent or monosyllabic ineffectuality has replaced chattering and braying, both ineffectual. Nothing has happened, because nothing has changed, and so this couple will be rubbed down to rubbish in the end. Is that enough to constitute a dramatic image? Albee, who began, in *The Zoo Story*, with the rhetorical strength and exacerbated vision of a strong dramatist, seems to have slain his own powers of representation almost before he himself can have understood them. *Who's Afraid of Virginia Woolf?*, whatever its impact upon contemporary audiences, clearly is of an age, and hardly for all time.

BRIAN WAY

Albee and the Absurd: The American Dream *and* The Zoo Story

As the American dramatist is often torn between a desire for the apparent security of realism and the temptation to experiment, so in Edward Albee's work, we see a tension between realism and the theatre of the absurd. *The Death of Bessie Smith* is a purely realistic play, and *Who's Afraid of Virginia Woolf?* is, for all its showiness, no more than a cross between sick drawing-room comedy and naturalistic tragedy. *The Zoo Story, The Sandbox* and *The American Dream* are, on the face of it, absurd plays, and yet, if one compares them with the work of Beckett, Ionesco or Pinter, they all retreat from the full implications of the absurd when a certain point is reached. Albee still believes in the validity of reason—that things can be proved, or that events can be shown to have definite meanings—and, unlike Beckett and the others, is scarcely touched by the sense of living in an absurd universe. Interesting and important as his plays are, his compromise seems ultimately a failure of nerve—a concession to those complementary impulses towards cruelty and self-pity which are never far below the surface of his work.

Albee has been attracted to the theatre of the absurd mainly, I think, because of the kind of social criticism he is engaged in. Both *The Zoo Story* and *The American Dream* are savage attacks on the American Way of Life. (I put the phrase in capitals to emphasize that this is not necessarily the way people in America actually live—simply that it is a pattern to which many Americans tend to conform, and, above all, that in the comics, on television, in advertising, and whenever an agency projects the personality of a poli-

From *American Theatre* (Stratford-upon-Avon Studies 10). © 1967 by Edward Arnold, Ltd., Edward Arnold (Publishers) Ltd., 1967.

tician, this is the way in which Americans are assumed and expected to live). Earlier satirists, like Sinclair Lewis and H. L. Mencken, had made their attack through a heightened, but basically realistic, picture of representative men and social habits—Babbitt and the business-world, Elmer Gantry and religion—but this method is no longer appropriate. The American Way of Life has become a political slogan and a commercial vested interest since the war, and is maintained and manipulated through a conscious process of image-building carried out mainly by the mass media of communication. A would-be social critic of today has to concern himself with these images rather than with representative men, and for the deflation of images realism is not necessarily the most effective artistic convention.

The American Way of Life, in the sense in which I am using the phrase, is a structure of images; and the images, through commercial and political exploitation, have lost much of their meaning. When the Eisenhower family at prayer becomes a televised political stunt, or the family meal an opportunity for advertising frozen foods, the image of the family is shockingly devalued. The deception practised is more complex than a simple lie: it involves a denial of our normal assumptions about evidence—about the relation between the observed world and its inner reality. This is why the techniques of the theatre of the absurd, which is itself preoccupied with the devaluation of language and of images, and with the deceptive nature of appearances, are so ideally suited to the kind of social criticism Albee intends. It is for this reason, too, that he has felt able to use the techniques of the theatre of the absurd, while stopping short of an acceptance of the metaphysic of the absurd upon which the techniques are based. It is possible, clearly, to see the absurd character of certain social situations without believing that the whole of life is absurd. In Albee's case, however, this has meant a restriction of scope, and his plays do not have the poetic quality or imaginative range of *Waiting for Godot*, for instance, or *The Caretaker*, or *Rhinoceros*.

The absurd, then, in so far as it interests the student of literature, presents itself for discussion on two levels: first, there is an underlying vision of the universe, a vision memorably expressed by Kafka and the existentialists as well as by the dramatists of the absurd; and secondly, a number of forms of writing and strategies of presentation generated by the underlying vision.

A writer's vision is absurd when the arbitrary, the disconnected, the irrelevant, non-reason, are seen to be the main principle or non-principle of the universe. Pascal, whom existentialists sometimes claim as a precursor, has expressed the vision most succinctly when he writes:

Je m'effraie et m'étonne de me voir ici plutôt que là, car il n'y a point de raison pourquoi ici plutôt que là, pourquoi à présent plutôt que lors.

[I am frightened and amazed to see myself here rather than there, since there is no reason at all why here rather than there, why now rather than then.]

Jean-Paul Sartre has the most complete and celebrated account of the experience in *La Nausée*, where Roquentin sits on a park bench and stares at the root of a chestnut tree. When, later, he tries to characterize the experience, the word Absurdity comes to him:

Un geste, un événement dans le petit monde calorié des hommes n'est jamais absurde que relativement: par rapport aux circonstances qui l'accompagnent. Les discours d'un fou, par exemple, sont absurdes par rapport à la situation où il se trouve mais non par rapport à son délire. Mais moi, tout à l'heure, j'ai fait l'expérience de l'absolu: l'absolu ou l'absurde. Cette racine, il n'y avait rien par rapport à quoi elle ne' fût absurde. . . . Absurde: par rapport aux cailloux, aux touffes d'herbe jaune, à la boue sèche, à l'arbre, au ciel, aux bancs verts. Absurde, irréductible; rien—pas même un délire profond et secret de la nature—ne pouvait l'expliquer. Evidemment je ne savais pas tout, je n'avais pas vu le germe se développer ni l'arbre croître. Mais devant cette grosse patte rugueuse, ni l'ignorance ni le savoir n'avait d'importance: le monde des explications et des raisons n'est pas celui de l'existence. J'avais beaue répéter: 'C'est une racine'—ça ne prenait plus. Je voyais bien qu'on ne pouvait pas passer de sa fonction de racine, de pompe aspirante, *à ça*, à cette peau dure et compacte de phoque, à cet aspect huileux, calleux, entêté. La fonction n'expliquait rien: elle permettait de comprendre en gros ce que c'était qu'une racine, mais pas du tout *celle-ci*.

[A gesture, an event, in the cosy little world of men is never absurd except relatively: in relation to the circumstances which accompany it. The words of a madman, for example, are only absurd in relation to the situation he is in, but not in relation to his delirium. But I, just now, experienced the absolute: the absolute or the absurd. There was nothing in relation to which this

root was not absurd. . . . Absurd: in relation to the pebbles, the
tufts of yellow grass, the dry mud, the tree, the sky, the green
benches. Absurd, irreducible: nothing—not even a profound secret delirium of nature—could explain it. Obviously I did not
know everything, I had not seen the seed develop, nor the tree
grow. But in front of this great gnarled foot, neither ignorance
nor knowledge had any importance: the world of explanations
and reasons is not that of existence . . . It was useless for me to
repeat: "It is a root"—that didn't fit any longer. I saw very well
that one could not move from its function as a root, as a suction
pump, *to that*, to that tough close seal's skin, to that greasy, horny,
stubborn appearance. Its function explained nothing: it allowed
one to understand in a general way what a root was, but not at
all what *this was*.]

Both Pascal and Sartre describe vividly the arbitrary, dislocated quality of
experience—the sense of living in a world where nothing has any fundamental connection with anything else. Sartre goes a stage further when he
exposes the irrelevance and the futility of reason—the reason in which the
naturalist writer has supreme faith—and the completely illusory nature of
rational explorations. When one says to oneself "It's a root" and continues
in a generalizing abstracting way to explain to oneself what it is that a root
does in relation to the tree and the earth, one is deceiving oneself if one
imagines that the process brings one any nearer to understanding *that*—that
object which is unique, stubborn (entêté), and, as Roquentin says a little
later, "beneath any possible explanation (au-dessous de toute explication)."
There is no transition from the world of explanations to the world of the
absurd; from the notion that a root is a suction pump to the thing itself—
the bark tough and close as a seal's skin, the greasy stubborn horny thing
before Roquentin's eyes.

A writer for whom experiences are as dislocated and unrelated as this
must clearly deny the logic of cause and effect, the logic on which naturalistic
drama is based. Sartre expresses this denial in a particularly interesting way
in the sequence of reflections from which I have already quoted:

Des arbres, des piliers bleu de nuit, le râle heureux d'une fontaine,
des odeurs vivantes, des petits brouillards de chaleur qui flottait
dans l'air froid, un homme roux qui digérait sur un banc: toutes
ces somnolences, toutes ces digestions prises ensemble offraient
un aspect vaguement comique. Comique . . . non: ça n'allait pas
jusque-là, rien de ce qui existe ne peut être comique; c'était comme

une analogie flottante, presque insaisissable avec certaines situations de vaudeville.

[Trees, midnight blue pillars, the happy chatter of a fountain, vivid scents, light warm vapours floating in the cold air, a red-haired man digesting his lunch on a bench: all this drowsing and digestion taken as a whole had a vaguely comic aspect. Comic . . . no, it didn't go quite as far as that, nothing which exists can be comic; it was like a fleeting analogy, almost impossible to grasp, with certain music-hall situations.]

"Comique . . . non . . . une analogie flottante . . . avec certaines situations de vaudeville"—incidents, that is, which have the logic of music-hall slapstick, but which are not necessarily funny. In music-hall acts and in the slapstick situations of the early cinema we see constantly this denial of the logic of cause and effect on which Sartre's analogy is based: in *City Lights* a statue is being unveiled; we expect a dignified climax to a public ceremony, but instead we find Chaplin cradled in the statue's arms making frantic efforts to climb down. Similarly in Ionesco's *Rhinoceros*, in which the citizens of a French provincial town are being rapidly transformed into rhinoceroses, the telephone rings, and Bérenger picks it up, with certain reasonable expectations as to whom his correspondent will be:

> BÉRENGER: Perhaps the authorities have decided to take action at last; maybe they're ringing to ask our help in whatever measures they've decided to adopt.
> DAISY: I'd be surprised if it was them.
> (*The telephone rings again.*)
> BÉRENGER: It is the authorities, I tell you, I recognize the ring—a long-drawn-out ring, I can't ignore an appeal from them. It can't be anyone else. (*He picks up the receiver.*) Hallo? (*Trumpetings are heard coming from the receiver.*) You hear that? Trumpeting! Listen!
> (*Daisy puts the telephone to her ear, is shocked by the sound, quickly replaces the receiver.*)
> DAISY [*frightened*]: What's going on?
> BÉRENGER: They're playing jokes now.
> DAISY: Jokes in bad taste!

Bérenger, an inveterate believer in the logic of cause and effect, a man who is certain he lives in a meaningful universe, picks up the telephone and instead of the reassuring voice of the authorities hears the trumpeting of rhinoceroses. It is indeed, as Daisy says, a joke in bad taste—"Comique . . . non . . . une analogie flottante . . . avec certaines situations de vaudeville." There could be no more vivid dramatic instance of what it means to live in an absurd universe.

The absurdist habit of mind, then, is overwhelmingly intellectualist, metaphysical even. It constantly asks the question "What is the meaning of life?", and finds as an answer, "There is no meaning," or, "We do not know," a discovery which may be horrifying or comic, or both. The theatre of the absurd has responded to this metaphysic by evolving new dramatic forms, and the second stage of my analysis of the absurd will be an examination of these.

For the playwright who accepts without reservations that he is living in an absurd universe, the loss of faith in reason which is at the heart of this vision and the conviction that the rational exploration of experience is a form of self-deception, imply a rejection of those theatrical conventions which reflect a belief in reason. Characters with fixed identities; events which have a definite meaning; plots which assume the validity of cause and effect; dénouements which offer themselves as complete resolutions of the questions raised by the play; and language which claims to mean what it says—none of these can be said to be appropriate means for expressing the dislocated nature of experience in an absurd world. In terms of formal experiment, then, the theatre of the absurd represents a search for images of non-reason.

Albee has used these images of non-reason in his attack on the American Way of Life without, as I have said, accepting the underlying vision which generated them. His work belongs to the second level of the theatre of the absurd: it shows a brilliantly inventive sense of what can be done with the techniques, but stops short of the metaphysic which makes the techniques completely meaningful. Nevertheless, *The American Dream* and *The Zoo Story* are the most exciting productions of the American theatre in the last fifteen years, and I propose to analyse them in detail in such a way as to bring out particularly what they have in common with other absurd plays and where they diverge from them.

In *The American Dream* (1961), Albee is closer to Ionesco than to any other dramatist. Like Ionesco, he sees the absurd localized most sharply in conventions of social behaviour. For both dramatists, the normal currency of social intercourse—of hospitality, or courtesy, or desultory chat—has lost its meaning, and this "devaluation of language," to use Martin Esslin's invaluable phrase, is an index for them of the vacuity of the social life represented. The inane civilities exchanged by the Smiths and the Martins in

The Bald Prima Donna [*The Bald Soprano*, U.S. title] enact the complete absence of human contact which is the reality beneath the appearance of communication. We see similar effects in *The American Dream* in the opening exchanges:

> DADDY: Uh . . . Mrs. Barker, is it? Won't you sit down?
>
> MRS. BARKER: I don't mind if I do.
>
> MOMMY: Would you like a cigarette, and a drink, and would you like to cross your legs?
>
> MRS. BARKER: You forget yourself, Mommy; I'm a professional woman. But I will cross my legs.
>
> DADDY: Yes, make yourself comfortable.
>
> MRS. BARKER: I don't mind if I do.

Ionesco and Albee use this method of exposing the essential meaninglessness of most middle-class language and gesture as a basis for much wider effects than the mere deflation of certain speech-habits. In Ionesco, particularly, it becomes a major principle of dramatic construction. He subjects conventional patterns of behaviour, the clichés of which much everyday speech is entirely composed, and the most complacent and unthinking of our normal assumptions and attitudes, to a disturbing shift of perspective: he places them in grotesque situations where they are ludicrously inappropriate, and their meaninglessness is stripped bare. *Amédée* (1954) is probably his most elaborate exercise in this technique. Amédée and Madeleine Buccinioni, a middle-aged bourgeois couple, have shut themselves up in their Paris apartment for fifteen years in order to conceal the corpse of a man Amédée may have murdered. The corpse has grown a white beard and long fingernails and toenails over the years, but during act 1, its rate of growth is suddenly accelerated, presenting Amédée and Madeleine with an acute problem:

> MADELEINE: The neighbours must have heard.
>
> AMÉDÉE [*stopping*]: They *may* not have done. [*Short silence.*] There's not a sound from them! . . . Besides, at this time of day . . .
>
> MADELEINE: They must have heard something. They're not all deaf . . .
>
> AMÉDÉE: Not *all* of them, they couldn't be. But as I say, at this time of day . . .
>
> MADELEINE: What could we tell them?
>
> AMÉDÉE: We could say it was the postman!

MADELEINE (*turning her back to the audience and looking towards the rear window*): It was the postman who did it! It was the p-o-stman! [*To* AMÉDÉE]: Will they believe us? The postman must have gone, by now.

AMÉDÉE: All the better. [*Loudly shouting to the rear of the stage*]. It was the p-o-stman!

MADELEINE:
AMÉDÉE: It was the p-o-stman! The p-o-stman!

[*They stop shouting, and the echo is heard.*]

ECHO: The p-o-stman! The p-o-stman! P-o-stman! O-o-stman!

AMÉDÉE [*he and* MADELEINE *both turning to face the audience*]: You see, even the echo is repeating it.

MADELEINE: Perhaps it isn't the echo!

AMÉDÉE: It strengthens our case, any how. It's an alibi! . . . Let's sit down.

MADELEINE [*sitting down*]: Life's really getting impossible. Where are we to find new window-panes?

[*Suddenly, from the adjoining room, a violent bang is heard against the wall;* AMÉDÉE, *who was about to sit down, stands up again, his gaze rivetted on the left of the stage;* MADELEINE *does the same.*]

MADELEINE [*uttering a cry*]: Ah!

AMÉDÉE [*distractedly*]: Keep calm, keep calm!

[*The left-hand door gradually gives way, as though under steady pressure.*]

MADELEINE [*not far from fainting, but still standing, cries out again*]: Ah, Heaven help us!

[*Then* AMÉDÉE *and* MADELEINE, *dumb with terror, watch two enormous feet slide slowly in through the open door and advance about eighteen inches on to the stage.*]

MADELEINE: Look!

[*This is naturally an anguished cry, yet there should be a certain restraint about it; it should, of course, convey fear, but above all, irritation. This is an embarrassing situation, but it should not seem at all unusual, and the actors should play this scene quite naturally. It is a "nasty blow" of course, an extremely "nasty blow," but no worse than that.*]

The dialogue is composed entirely of clichés, and is dominated by mundane bourgeois attitudes—chiefly the anxiety to preserve appearances before neighbours, and the desperate determination to act as if everything were normal. (Ionesco's final stage direction, of course, underlines this.) As so often in absurd drama, the language and the action contradict each other. The grotesque horror of the situation is played off against the ludicrous pretence at maintaining a sense of the ordinary suggested by the language. When middle-class clichés and stock attitudes are shown to be so evidently meaningless in this situation, one is directed to the conclusion that they are in fact meaningless in all situations, and that only the blindness of habit conceals this fact from us.

Albee develops the situation in *The American Dream* along similar lines. He sees the American Way of Life as one in which normal human feelings and relationships have been deprived of meaning. The gestures of love, sexual attraction, parental affection, family feeling and hospitality remain, but the actual feelings which would give the gestures meaning have gone. To show this in sharp dramatic terms, Albee constructs a situation of gestures which are normally supposed to have meaning but, as transposed by him, are seen to have none. As soon as the family tableau of Mommy and Daddy, the overtly homey middle-aged couple, and Grandma, their apparent tribute to the duty of caring for the aged, is presented, we see what Albee is doing:

MOMMY: We were very poor! But then I married you, Daddy, and now we're very rich.

DADDY: Grandma isn't rich.

MOMMY: No, but you've been so good to Grandma she feels rich. She doesn't know you'd like to put her in a nursing home.

DADDY: I wouldn't!

MOMMY: Well, heaven knows *I* would! I can't stand it, watching her do the cooking and the housework, polishing the silver, moving the furniture. . . .

DADDY: She likes to do that. She says it's the least she can do to earn her keep.

MOMMY: Well, she's right. You can't live off people . . . I have a right to live off you because I married you, and because I used to let you get on top of me and bump your uglies; and I have a right to all your money when you die. And when you do, Grandma and I can live by ourselves . . . if she's still here. Unless you have her put away in a nursing home.

DADDY: I have no intention of putting her in a nursing home.

> MOMMY: Well, I wish somebody would do something with her!
> DADDY: At any rate you're very well provided for.
> MOMMY: You're my sweet Daddy; that's very nice.
> DADDY: I love my Mommy.

The characters are isolated from each other in little worlds of selfishness, impotence and lovelessness, and all warmth of human contact is lost. It would be inaccurate to say that the gestures of love and connection ("You're my sweet Daddy"—"I love my Mommy") are deflated; their meaninglessness is exposed by tagging them on as afterthoughts to phases of the action where they are—as here—ludicrously inapplicable.

This method of scene construction determines not only the local effects of *The American Dream*, but the major patterns of the play. Albee is disturbed and agonized by the extent of the dislocation of people's relationships and the imprisoning isolation of which these scenes are images. The play's central image of this failure of human feeling and contact is sterility—the inability to beget or bear a child—and as its title suggests, Albee tries to give the image the widest possible social reference. He implies that the sterility which the audience sees in his characters is typical of the society as a whole, and is created and perpetuated by the society. For him, the American Way of Life systematically eliminates, in the name of parental care, and social and moral concern, every trace of natural human feeling and every potentiality for warm human contact from those who have to live by it, and especially from the young.

When Mommy, Daddy and Grandma, and the quality of their lives, have been firmly established, Mrs. Barker, a representative of the Bye-Bye Adoption Service, calls on them. She forgets why she has called (a common motif in absurd plays, underlining the arbitrariness and irrelevance of all action in an absurd world, though little more than a gimmick here). Grandma, to help her, gives her a "hint"—the story of "a man very much like Daddy, and a woman very much like Mommy," and "a dear lady" very much like Mrs. Barker. It is a story of individual sterility:

> The woman who was very much like Mommy, said that she and the man who was very much like Daddy had never been blessed with anything very much like a bumble of joy. . . .
>
> [S]he said that they wanted a bumble of their own, but that the man, who was very much like Daddy, couldn't have a bumble; and the man, who was very much like Daddy, said that yes, they had wanted a bumble of their own, but that the woman, who was very much like Mommy, couldn't have one and that now they wanted to buy something very much like a bumble.

It is also a story of that collective sterility which eliminates natural impulses in others. Mommy and Daddy buy "a bumble of joy," and its upbringing is a series of mutilations at their hands:

> GRANDMA: . . . *then*, it began to develop an interest in its you-know-what.
>
> MRS. BARKER: In its you-know-what! Well! I hope they cut its hands off at the wrists!
>
> GRANDMA: Well, yes, they did that eventually. But first, they cut off its you-know-what.
>
> MRS. BARKER: A much better idea!
>
> GRANDMA: That's what they thought. But after they cut off its you-know-what, it *still* put its hands under the covers, *looking* for its you-know-what. So, finally, they had to cut off its hands at the wrists.

The child's eyes are gouged out, it is castrated, its hands are cut off, its tongue is cut out, and finally it dies. In this brilliant sequence of dramatic writing, Albee has given us a fable of his society, where all the capabilities for connection—eyes to see, sexual organs with which to love, hands to touch, and tongue to speak—are destroyed, and the victim of the socializing processes of the American Way of Life, humanly speaking, dies. And it is all done in the name of affection and care. Once again, the gestures of human contact survive grotesquely in the coyness with which the sexual act and the begetting and rearing of children are described ("being blessed with a bumble of joy," "its you-know-what") and the gestures are seen to be hideously and mockingly at odds with the reality.

Towards the end of the play, the victim himself appears—the "twin" of "the bumble of joy." He is a young man with all the external marks of youth and vitality, handsome, muscular and self-confident. Grandma recognizes in him immediately the American Dream. But just as the gestures of parental love have been only a sham, his outwardly vigorous youthful appearance is only a shell. His life is a terrible emptiness, a series of deprivations identical with the mutilations practised on his "twin" brother:

> I don't know what became of my brother . . . to the rest of myself . . . except that, from time to time, in the years that have passed, I have suffered losses . . . that I can't explain. A fall from grace . . . a departure of innocence . . . loss . . . loss. . . . Once . . . it was as if all at once my heart . . . became numb . . . almost as though I . . . almost as though . . . just like that . . . it had been wrenched from my body . . . and from that time I have been unable to love.

> And there is more . . . there are more losses, but it all comes down to this: I no longer have the capacity to feel anything. I have no emotions. I have been drained, torn asunder . . . disembowelled. I have, now, only my person . . . my body, my face. I use what I have . . . I let people love me . . . I accept the syntax around me, for while I cannot relate . . . I know I must be related *to*.

This moving speech is one of those moments of total illumination in absurd drama (Aston's account of his experiences in the psychiatric ward in *The Caretaker* is the finest example) where a character, for a moment, sees the entire hopelessness and confusion of his existence before lapsing once more into the "syntax around" him. The Young Man has to accept that syntax—the meaningless gestures of human affection and contact—when he is adopted, or re-adopted, by Mommy and Daddy. While they celebrate with Sauterne, Grandma observes sardonically from the wings: "Well, I guess that just about wraps it up. I mean, for better or worse, this is a comedy. . . ." The bad Sauterne is drunk, and sterility, impotence, lovelessness, and disconnection are masked with the gestures of celebration, conviviality and family-love, suggesting as they do all that is lacking—the physical warmth of sex and parenthood, and the meaningfulness of people being together. Only the gestures remain, these gestures which have been simultaneously canonized and deprived of meaning by the publicists of the American Way of Life: the politicians, the admen, the columnists and the TV commentators.

It is significant that the only character in *The American Dream* with any vitality or attractiveness is Grandma—and she is "rural," from an older way of life. The way in which she is juxtaposed against the Young Man who is the American Dream seems to symbolize a society in which the natural order of life has been reversed, in which the younger one is, the less chance one has of being alive.

These patterns and images occur elsewhere in Albee's work. His sense of human isolation and despair is the central preoccupation of *The Death of Bessie Smith* (a bad play, it seems to me), and in *The Sandbox*, which parallels the situation of *The American Dream* most interestingly, though on too cramped a stage. The image of sterility is very prominent in *Who's Afraid of Virginia Woolf?*, but is used there much less effectively than in *The American Dream*. Apart from its spectacular ability to amuse and shock, *Virginia Woolf* has a certain emptiness—no incident or image in it has reference to anything wider than the neuroses of its characters.

His first play, *The Zoo Story* (1959), however, contains some very fine dramatic writing. Again it is an exploration of the farce and the agony of human isolation. When the play opens, Peter, a prosperous youngish man in the publishing business, is reading on a bench in Central Park, New York. Jerry, who describes himself as a "permanent transient," insists on talking to Peter. Peter tries to brush him off, to get on with his reading, but Jerry forces Peter to confront him fully as a human being, working first on his curiosity, and then provoking him by insults and blows. When Peter is sufficiently enraged, they fight. Jerry, in an improbable and sentimental catastrophe, puts a knife in Peter's hand and impales himself on it. He succeeds in forcing Peter out from behind the shelter of his possessions (symbolized by the park bench over which they ostensibly fight) and his middle-class complacency, into a real confrontation with the isolation and despair of the human condition. If Jerry is a "permanent transient," Peter is, after the killing, at least "dispossessed":

> You won't be coming back here any more, Peter; you've been dispossessed. You've lost your bench, but you've defended your honor.

And Jerry, in turn, even if it has cost him his life, has at last made "contact" with another being.

It is because human isolation is so great, and because the "contact" which would end it is so formidably difficult to obtain, that Jerry went to the zoo:

> Now I'll let you in on what happened at the zoo; but first, I should tell you why I went to the zoo. I went to the zoo to find out more about the way people exist with animals, and the way animals exist with each other, and with people too. It probably wasn't a fair test, what with everyone separated by bars from everyone else, the animals for the most part from each other, and always the people from the animals. But if it's a zoo, that's the way it is.

The entire human condition, for Jerry, is a zoo story of people (and animals) forever separated by bars.

In its finest scene, the long speech in which Jerry describes his attempt to form a relationship with his landlady's dog, *The Zoo Story* offers a superb example of what I call pseudo-crisis—the second pattern of absurd writing that is central to Albee's work. In classic drama, crisis is one of the most important means by which the action is significantly advanced. In *Othello*,

for instance, when Iago tells Othello that he has seen Desdemona's handkerchief in Cassio's hands, a whole complex of tensions is brought to a head,
and after this crisis, the catastrophe is measurably nearer, and Othello is
demonstrably a stage further on his course of violence and madness. In the
absurd play, on the other hand, what I call a pseudo-crisis occurs when a
similar complex of tensions is brought to a head without resolving anything,
without contributing to any development or progression, serving in fact to
demonstrate that nothing as meaningful as progression or development can
occur, emphasizing that complexity and tension are permanent and unresolvable elements of a world of confusion. Lucky's speech in *Waiting for
Godot* is perhaps the most elaborate and extreme occurrence. Harold Pinter's
work, too, is full of pseudo-crisis, the funniest instance, perhaps, being
Davies's account of his visit to the monastery at Luton in search of boots
(*The Caretaker*).

Jerry's long speech in *The Zoo Story* has all the marks of pseudo-crisis.
It is used here to explore Albee's preoccupation with man's failure to make
contact with others, and the drying up of those feelings that should provide
connection. Jerry lives in a rooming house where the landlady's dog attacks
him every time he comes in. He is fascinated by the dog's hatred; he responds
to it with obsessive force: it is a challenge—the dog is intensely concerned
about him and if he can meet the challenge he may be able to create out of
it the contact he is looking for. He decides that first he will try to kill the
dog with kindness, and if that fails he will simply kill it. He feeds it ham-
burgers; its animosity doesn't diminish, and so, at the climax of this pseudo-
crisis—a farcical and yet poignant parody of the love-hate situation in romantic fiction—he gives the dog a poisoned hamburger. Nothing really
happens, nothing is resolved. The dog doesn't die, nor does it come to love
Jerry; for a moment Jerry and the dog look at each other, but then the dog
withdraws from contact with him; even the pressure of its hatred has gone—
"We neither love nor hurt because we do not try to reach each other," Jerry
says, trying to express the agony of his need:

> I loved the dog now, and I wanted him to love me. I had tried
> to love and I had tried to kill, and both had been unsuccessful
> by themselves. . . . I hoped that the dog would understand.
>
> It's just that if you can't deal with people, you have to make
> a start somewhere. WITH ANIMALS! (*much faster now, and like a
> conspirator*) . . . Don't you see? A person has to have some way
> of dealing with SOMETHING. If not with people . . . SOMETHING.
> With a bed, with a cockroach, with a mirror . . . no, that's too

hard, that's one of the last steps. With a cockroach, with a . . . with a . . . with a carpet, with a roll of toilet paper . . . no, not that either . . . that's a mirror, too; always check bleeding. You see how hard it is to find things? With a street corner, and too many lights, all colours reflecting on the oily-wet streets . . . with a wisp of smoke, a wisp . . . of smoke . . . with . . . with . . . with love, with vomiting, with crying, with fury because the pretty little ladies aren't pretty little ladies, with making money with your body which is an act of love and I could prove it, with howling because you're alive; with God. How about that? WITH GOD WHO IS A COLOURED QUEEN WHO WEARS A KIMONO AND PLUCKS HIS EYEBROWS, WHO IS A WOMAN WHO CRIES WITH DETERMINATION BEHIND HER CLOSED DOOR . . . with God, who, I'm told, turned his back on the whole thing some time ago . . . with . . . some day, with people . . . (JERRY *sighs the next word heavily*) People. With an idea; a concept. And where better, where ever better in this humiliating excuse for a jail, where better to communicate one single, simple-minded idea than in an entrance-hall? Where? It would be a START! Where better to make a beginning . . . to understand and just possibly be understood . . . than with . . . than with A DOG. Just that; a dog . . . A dog.

The dramatic structure of this part of Jerry's speech reflects very closely the rhythms of pseudo-crisis—the excitement, the tensions, rising to the shouted climax ("WITH GOD WHO IS . . ."), and then slipping away into the lax despairing tempo of its inconclusive end ("with . . . some day, with people"). The hopelessness of this is quickly recognized, and Jerry reverts to his attempt with the dog, but this, too, has failed and proved nothing. In this final downward curve of the pseudo-crisis everything is conditional and hypothetical ("It would be A START! Where better to make a beginning . . . to understand, and just possibly be understood . . .").

In this early play, there is an attempt, too, to relate Jerry's agony to the wider social pattern—to see it as a product of the American Way of Life:

> I am a *permanent transient*, and my home is in the sickening rooming-houses on the West Side of New York City, which is the greatest city in the world. Amen.

In spite of the bitter force of this, however, it is clear that the impulse of social criticism has only been very partially translated into dramatic terms. Jerry's outburst here tells the audience how to react; it is almost a piece of editorializing, and doesn't have the persuasiveness of art, the sense that ideas have become vision and are being enacted.

At such moments in *The Zoo Story*, and most of all, of course, at the moment of Jerry's melodramatic and sentimental death, we are left with a sense of dissatisfaction whose root causes are to be found in that compromise with the experimental theatre that seems to me so characteristic of American dramatists. The action and the dialogue are dislocated, arbitrary and absurd (pre-eminently in Jerry's story of the dog) up to the moment of Jerry's death, and then all the traditional assumptions of naturalism flood back into the play. It is postulated, quite as firmly as in any Ibsen social drama, that a catastrophe is also a resolution of the situation of the play, and that events, however obscure, ultimately have a definite and unambiguous meaning. Jerry spends his dying breath telling us what the play means as explicitly as does Lona Hessel at the end of *Pillars of Society*. This sudden reversion to a faith in the validity of rational explanations makes previous events in the play seem arbitrary in a wholly unjustifiable way: they can no longer be seen as appropriate symbols of life in an absurd universe. The slightest hint that events in an absurd play are amenable to everyday explanation is completely destructive of their dramatic effectiveness. If it were possible to say of Vladimir and Estragon, or of Davies, that they are crazy bums who should be locked up, *Waiting for Godot* and *The Caretaker* would be ruined. In spite of some striking effects, it is possible to entertain this suspicion about Jerry, and it is largely because of this misguided attempt to exploit the advantages both of the theatre of the absurd and of realism, that *The Zoo Story* misses the greatness which at times seems so nearly within its grasp.

The American Dream does not show so straightforward an evasion of the absurd as *The Zoo Story*, but it lacks even more completely the metaphysical dimension. One can perhaps best begin accounting for its limitations by noting a distinction which Martin Esslin makes most perceptively: first there is—

> The experience that Ionesco expresses in plays like *The Bald Prima Donna* or *The Chairs*, Adamov in *La Parodie*, or N. F. Simpson in *A Resounding Tinkle*. It represents the satirical, parodistic aspect of the Theatre of the Absurd, its social criticism, its pillorying of an inauthentic, petty society. This may be the most easily accessible, and therefore most widely recognized, message of the Theatre of the Absurd, but it is far from being its most essential or most significant feature.
>
> Behind the satirical exposure of the absurdity of inauthentic ways of life, the Theatre of the Absurd is facing up to a deeper

layer of absurdity—the absurdity of the human condition itself in a world where the decline of religious belief has deprived man of certainties.

The American Dream is effective only within the limits of the first category. It is too exclusively and merely a satire of American middle-class aspirations and self-deceptions. It is, above all, a play about Other People, not about ourselves: when we laugh at Mommy and Daddy, we are laughing at emotional and sexual failures which we do not recognize as our own and in which we refuse to be implicated, whereas when we laugh at Davies, or at Vladimir and Estragon, we are laughing at our own illusions and recognizing our own acts of hubris, self-deception and failure. Since *The American Dream* doesn't implicate us, it never becomes tragic. Harold Pinter has said of his own play:

> As far as I am concerned *The Caretaker* is funny up to a point. Beyond that point it ceases to be funny, and it was because of that point that I wrote it.

Albee never reached this point except perhaps for the brief moment I have noted where the Young Man's sense of loss is met with Grandma's compassion. But we do not otherwise have to regard the characters—certainly not Mommy and Daddy—as tragic or even terrifying: they enact for us a certain attitude to America in 1960; they do not go beyond it to tell us anything about the human condition.

In one important sense, *The American Dream* does not belong even to the "satirical, parodistic" category of absurd plays. It is, like *The Zoo Story*, a play which reaches a definite conclusion and which implicitly claims that its events have an unambiguous meaning. Grandma's "hint" to Mrs. Barker is a fable of almost diagrammatic directness and simplicity; by contrast, the Fireman's fables in *The Bald Prima Donna* are absurd parodies, satirizing the assumption that a tale has a "moral," and further, undermining our confidence in the kind of popular wisdom represented by the morals of Aesop's fables.

Above all, at the end of *The American Dream*, Grandma can tell the audience:

> Well, I guess that just about wraps it up. I mean, for better or worse, this is a comedy, and I don't think we'd better go any further. No, definitely not. So let's leave things as they are right now . . . while everybody's happy . . . while everybody's got what he wants . . . or everybody's got what he thinks he wants. Good night, dears.

Her remark, "Well, I guess that just about wraps it up," is ironical only in the most external sense—in the sense that Mommy and Daddy and the Young Man and Mrs. Barker, who have all just drunk "To satisfaction," are in for some unpleasant surprises. As far as Grandma and the audience are concerned the situation really is wrapped up, and the play has proved its point as self-consciously as any theorem. Again, *The Bald Prima Donna* is a significant contrast, ending not with a proof but returning in a circle to the point at which it began.

It is only when one compares *The American Dream* with the greatest absurd plays that the real damage done by this compromise between reason and the absurd can be fully reckoned. In the first place, many of the local effects seem to be, in retrospect, merely tricks. The way in which it handles argument will illustrate what I mean. The metaphysic of the absurd, as I have said, involves a loss of faith in reason and in the validity of rational explorations of experience, and one of the most characteristic forms of writing of the absurd theatre, developed to represent this on the stage, is the systematic pursuit of the irrelevant. Absurd plays are full of arguments which lead nowhere, or which parody the processes of logic, or which are conducted from ludicrous premises. At the beginning of *The American Dream* Mommy's account of her argument in the department store as to whether her hat was beige or wheat-coloured is a clear instance of this. But it does not symbolize anything deeper: far from being an index of a world in which everything is too uncertain to be settled by argument, it takes its place in a play which, from its determination to prove a point, is naïvely confident in the power of argument. It therefore seems, in retrospect, no more than a trick to get the play started. By comparison, the argument in *Rhinoceros*, as to whether the animals which charged down the street had one horn or two, is funnier and also infinitely more disturbing: it represents the last feeble efforts of ordinary men to cling to their reassuring certitudes as their world founders into chaos, and, as they themselves, through turning into rhinoceroses, are about to lose their very identities. Albee's work lacks this imaginative dimension, to say nothing of the compassion, horror, and despair implicit in the periodic speculations of Vladimir and Estragon on the nature of Godot.

But it is in dénouements, as I have pointed out, that Albee diverges most clearly from the absurd, and it is here that the divergence does him most harm. His plays are tightly "wrapped up," where the best absurd plays leave us with an extended sense of uncertainties of our condition. The quiet heartrending close of *Waiting for Godot*—

> VLADIMIR: Well, shall we go?
> ESTRAGON: Yes, let's go.
>
> *They do not move.*

—or the end of *The Caretaker*, where Davies and Aston look ahead into their bleak future, a future in which Davies will never "get settled down and fixed up," and in which Aston will never build his shed, have all the dramatic and poetic power Albee lacks. Perhaps the most relevant comparison is with the lyrical closing moments of *Amédée*, where Amédée, as he floats up into the sky, makes a speech to the crowd:

> Ladies and Gentlemen . . . Please don't think . . . I should like
> to stay . . . stay with my feet on the ground . . . It's against my
> will . . . I don't want to get carried away . . . I'm all for progress,
> I like to be of use to my fellow men . . . I believe in social realism.

As well as being delightfully comic, Amédée's flight into space even while he utters all the positivist nostrums by which man tries to keep his feet on the ground, is an exquisite poetic image, where Albee's narrow cocksureness is poetically dead.

When all these limitations of scope have been noted, however, it is only fair that one should return to an assertion of the importance of Albee's good qualities in the American theatre. If it is true that he inhabits a finite world, he does so with brilliance, inventiveness, intelligence and moral courage.

GERALD WEALES

Edward Albee: Don't Make Waves

Something tells me it's all
happenin' at the zoo.
—Simon and Garfunkel

Edward Albee is inescapably *the* American playwright of the 1960's. His first play, *The Zoo Story*, opened in New York, on a double bill with Samuel Beckett's *Krapp's Last Tape*, at the Provincetown Playhouse on January 14, 1960. In his Introduction to *Three Plays* (1960), Albee tells how his play, which was written in 1958, passed from friend to friend, from country to country, from manuscript to tape to production (in Berlin in 1959) before it made its way back to the United States. "It's one of those things a person has to do," says Jerry; "sometimes a person has to go a very long distance out of his way to come back a short distance correctly."

For Albee, once *The Zoo Story* had finished its peregrinations, the trip uptown—psychologically and geographically—was a short one. During 1960, there were two other Albee productions, largely unheralded—*The Sandbox*, which has since become a favorite for amateurs, and *Fam and Yam*, a *bluette*, a joke growing out of his having been ticketed as the latest white hope of the American theater. These were essentially fugitive productions of occasional pieces. In 1961, one of the producers of *The Zoo Story*, Richard Barr, joined by Clinton Wilder in the producing organization that is always called Theater 196? after whatever the year, offered *The American Dream*, first on a double bill with William Flanagan's opera *Bartleby*, for which Albee and James Hinton, Jr., did the libretto, and later, when the opera proved

From *The Jumping-Off Place: American Drama in the 1960s.* © 1969 by Gerald Weales. The Macmillan Company, Collier-Macmillan Ltd., 1969.

unsuccessful, with an earlier Albee play *The Death of Bessie Smith*. During the next few years, there were frequent revivals of both *Zoo* and *Dream*, often to help out a sagging Barr-Wilder program, as in 1964 (by which time Albee had become a co-producer) when first *Dream* and later *Zoo* were sent in as companion pieces to LeRoi Jones's *Dutchman*, after Samuel Beckett's *Play* and Fernando Arrabal's *The Two Executioners*, which opened with Jones's play, were removed from the bill. Albee had become an off-Broadway staple.

By that time, of course, Albee had become something else as well. With *Who's Afraid of Virginia Woolf?* (1962), he had moved to Broadway and had a smashing commercial success. By a process of escalation, he had passed from promising to established playwright. After *Woolf*, Albee productions averaged one a year: *The Ballad of the Sad Café* (1963), *Tiny Alice* (1964), *Malcolm* (1966), *A Delicate Balance* (1966) and *Everything in the Garden* (1967). None of these were successes in Broadway terms (by *Variety*'s chart of hits and flops), but except for *Malcolm*, a gauche and imperceptive adaptation of James Purdy's novel of that name, which closed after seven performances, all of them had respectable runs and generated their share of admiration and antagonism from critics and public alike.

Although favorable reviews helped make the Albee reputation, critics have consistently praised with one hand, damned with the other. If Harold Clurman's "Albee on Balance" (*The New York Times*, January 13, 1967) treats Albee as a serious playwright and if Robert Brustein's "A Third Theater" (*The New York Times Magazine*, September 25, 1966) seems to dismiss him as a solemn one, only Broadway serious, the recent collections of their reviews—Clurman's *The Naked Image* and Brustein's *Seasons of Discontent*—indicate that both critics have had the same kind of reservations about Albee from the beginning. Albee, contrariwise, has had reservations of his own. From his pettish introduction to *The American Dream* to the press conference he called to chastise the critics for their reactions to *Tiny Alice*, he has regularly used interviews and the occasional nondramatic pieces he has written to suggest that the critics lack understanding, humility, responsibility.

In spite of (perhaps because of) the continuing quarrel between Albee and his critics—a love-hate relationship in the best Albee tradition—the playwright's reputation has grown tremendously. It was in part the notoriety of *Who's Afraid of Virginia Woolf?* that turned Albee into a popular figure, and certainly the publicity surrounding the making of the movie version of *Woolf* helped to keep Albee's name in the popular magazines. Whatever the cause, Albee is now the American playwright whose name has become a touchstone, however ludicrously it is used. Thus, Thomas Meehan, writing an article on "camp" for *The New York Times Magazine* (March 21, 1965), solicits Andy Warhol's opinion of *Tiny Alice* ("I liked it because it was so empty"), and William H. Honan, interviewing Jonathan Miller for the same publication (January 22, 1967), manages to get Miller to repeat a common-place criticism of Albee he has used twice before.

All this is simply the chi-chi mask over a serious concern with Albee. According to recent reports of the American Educational Theatre Associa-tion, Albee has been jockeying for second place (after Shakespeare) in the list of playwrights most produced on college campuses. In 1963–64, he held second place; in 1964–65, he was nosed out by Ionesco. The attractiveness of short plays to college dramatic groups—as Ionesco's presence suggests—helps explain the volume of Albee productions, but, with *The Zoo Story* invading text anthologies and *Virginia Woolf* climbing onto reading lists, it is clear that the interest in Albee in colleges is more than a matter of me-chanics. More and more articles on Albee turn up in critical quarterlies—always a gauge of academic fashions—and those that are printed are only the tip of a happily submerged iceberg; Walter Meserve, one of the editors of *Modern Drama*, estimated in 1966 that 80 per cent of the submissions on American drama were about four authors: O'Neill, Williams, Miller, and Albee. The interest abroad is as intense as it is here. This is clear not only from the fact that the plays are translated and performed widely, but in the desire of audiences to talk or to hear about the playwright. Clurman, in that article in the *Times*, reporting on lecture audiences in Tokyo and Tel Aviv, says that there was more curiosity about Albee than any other American playwright. Albee's position, then, is analogous to that of Tennessee Williams in the 1950's. He recognizes this himself. When he wrote *Fam and Yam* in 1960, he let Yam (the Young American Playwright) bunch Albee with Jack Gelber, Jack Richardson, and Arthur Kopit. In an interview in *Diplomat* (October, 1966) he suggested that playwrights should be hired as critics; it was now Williams and Arthur Miller that he listed with himself.

In "Which Theatre Is the Absurd One?" (*The New York Times Magazine*, February 25, 1962), Albee wrote that "in the end a public will get what it deserves and no better." If he is right, his work may finally condemn or justify the taste of American theater audiences in the 1960s. More than likely, a little of both.

"I consider myself in a way the most eclectic playwright who ever wrote," Albee once told an interviewer (*Translatlantic Review*, Spring, 1963), and then he went on to make an elaborate joke about how he agreed with the critics that twenty-six playwrights—three of whom he had never read—had influenced him. Critics do have a way of getting influence-happy when they write about Albee—particularly Brustein, who persists in calling him

an imitator—but they have good reason. There are such strong surface dis-
similarities among the Albee plays that it is easier and in some ways more
rewarding to think of *The Zoo Story* in relation to Samuel Beckett and Harold
Pinter and *A Delicate Balance* in terms of T. S. Eliot and Enid Bagnold than
it is to compare the two plays, even though both start from the same dramatic
situation: the invasion (by Jerry, by Harry and Edna) of private territory
(Peter's bench, Tobias's house). Yet, the comparison is obvious once it is
made. Each new Albee play seems to be an experiment in form, in style
(even if it is someone else's style), and yet there is unity in his work as a
whole. This is apparent in the devices and the characters that recur, modified
according to context, but it is most obvious in the repetition of theme, in
the basic assumptions about the human condition that underlie all his work.

In *A Delicate Balance*, Tobias and his family live in a mansion in the
suburbs of hell, that existential present so dear to contemporary writers, in
which life is measured in terms of loss, love by its failure, contact by its
absence. In that hell, there are many mansions—one of which is Peter's
bench—and all of them are cages in the great zoo story of life. Peter's bench
is a kind of sanctuary, both a refuge from and an extension of the stereotypical
upper-middle-class existence (tweeds, horn-rimmed glasses, job in publishing, well-furnished apartment, wife, daughters, cats, parakeets) with which
Albee has provided him—a place where he can safely not-live and have his
nonbeing. This is the way Jerry sees Peter, at least, and—since the type is
conventional enough in contemporary theater, from avant-garde satire to
Broadway revue—it is safe to assume that the play does, too. Although
Albee intends a little satirical fun at Peter's expense (the early needling scenes
are very successful), it is clear that the stereotyping of Peter is an image of
his condition, not a cause of it. Jerry, who plays "the old pigeonhole bit" so
well, is another, a contrasting cliché, and it is the play's business to show
that he and Peter differ only in that he does not share Peter's complacency.
Just before Jerry attacks in earnest, he presents the play's chief metaphor:

> I went to the zoo to find out more about the way people exist
> with animals, and the way animals exist with each other, and
> with people too. It probably wasn't a fair test, what with everyone
> separated by bars from everyone else, the animals for the most
> part from each other, and always the people from the animals.
> But, if it's a zoo, that's the way it is.

"Private wings," says Malcolm in the play that bears his name. "Indeed,
that *is* an extension of separate rooms, is it not?" In a further extension of a
joke that is no joke, Agnes, in *A Delicate Balance*, speaks of her "poor parents,

in their separate heavens." *Separateness* is the operative word for Albee characters, for, even though his zoo provides suites for two people (*Who's Afraid of Virginia Woolf?*) or for more (*A Delicate Balance*), they are furnished with separate cages. "It's sad to know you've gone through it all, or most of it, without . . ." says Edna in one of the fragmented speeches that characterize *A Delicate Balance*, as though thoughts too were separate, "that the one body you've wrapped your arms around . . . the only skin you've ever known . . . is your own—and that it's dry . . . and not warm." This is a more restrained, a more resigned variation on the Nurse's desperate cry in *Bessie Smith*, ". . . I am tired of my skin. . . . I WANT OUT!"

Violence is one of the ways of trying to get out. The Nurse is an illustration of this possibility; she is an embryonic version of Martha in *Virginia Woolf*, with most of the venom, little of the style, and practically none of the compensating softness of the later character, and she hits out at everyone around her. Yet, she never escapes herself, her cage. The other possibility is love (that, too, a form of penetration), but the Albee plays are full of characters who cannot (Nick in *Virginia Woolf*) or will not (Tobias, the Nurse) make that connection. The persistent images are of withdrawal, the most graphic being the one in *A Delicate Balance*, the information that Tobias in fact withdrew and came on Agnes's belly the last time they had sex. Although failed sex is a convenient metaphor for the failure of love, its opposite will not work so well. Connection is not necessarily contact, and it is contact—or rather its absence, those bars that bother Jerry—that preoccupies Albee. He lets Martha and George make fun of the lack-of-communication cliché in *Virginia Woolf*, but it is that cultural commonplace on which much of Albee's work is built. Jerry's story about his landlady's vicious dog—although he over-explains it—is still Albee's most effective account of an attempt to get through those bars, out of that skin (so effective, in fact, that Tobias uses a variation of it in *Balance* when he tells about his cat). Accepting the dog's attacks on him as a form of recognition, Jerry tries first to win his affection (with hamburger) and, failing that, to kill him (with poisoned hamburger: it is difficult to differentiate between the tools of love and hate). In the end, he settles for an accommodation, one in which he and the dog ignore each other. His leg remains unbitten, but he feels a sense of loss in the working arrangement: "We neither love nor hurt because we do not try to reach each other."

"Give me *any* person . . ." says Lawyer in *Tiny Alice*. "He'll take what he gets for . . . what he wishes it to be. AH, it is what I have always wanted, he'll say, looking terror and betrayal straight in the eye. Why not: face the inevitable and call it what you have always wanted." The context is a special one here, a reference to Julian's impending martyrdom to God-Alice, who comes to him in the form or forms he expects. I purposely dropped from the Lawyer's speech the references to "martyr" and "saint" which follow parenthetically after the opening phrase, for as it stands above, the speech might serve as advertising copy for the Albee world in which his characters exist and—very occasionally—struggle. The too-obvious symbol of *The American Dream*, the muscle-flexing young man who is only a shell, empty of love or feeling, is, in Mommy's words, "a great deal more like it." *Like it*, but not *it*. Appearance is what she wants, for reality, as Grandma's account of the mutilation of the other "bumble" indicates, is dangerous.

The American Dream is a pat example of, to use Lawyer's words again, "How to come out on top, going under." Whether the accommodation is embraced (*Dream*) or accepted with a sense of loss (Jerry and the dog), it is always there, a way of coping instead of a way of life. It can be disguised in verbal trappings—comic (the games in *Virginia Woolf*) or serious (the religiosity of *Tiny Alice*, the conventional labels of *A Delicate Balance*). In the absence of substance, it can be given busy work; Girard Girard spells everything out in *Malcolm*: "You will move from the mansion to the chateau, and from the chateau back. You will surround yourself with your young beauties, and hide your liquor where you will. You will . . . go on, my dear." The unhidden liquor in *A Delicate Balance* (even more in *Virginia Woolf*, where it serves the dramatic action, as lubricant and as occasional rest) provides an example of such busyness: all the playing at bartending, the weighty deliberation over whether to have anisette or cognac, the concern over the quality of a martini. The rush of words (abuse or elegance) and the press of activity (however meaningless) sustain the Albee characters in a tenuous relationship (a delicate balance) among themselves and in the face of the others, the ones outside, and—beyond that—the nameless terror.

Implicit in my discussion of the separateness of the Albee characters and the bogus forms of community they invent to mask the fact that they are alone is the assumption that this is Albee's view of the human condition. The deliberate refusal to locate the action of his most recent plays (*Tiny Alice*, *Malcolm*, *A Delicate Balance*) strengthens that assumption. In fact, only two of Albee's settings can be found in atlases—Central Park (*The Zoo Story*) and Memphis (*Bessie Smith*). Even these, like the undifferentiated Southern town he borrowed from Carson McCullers for *The Ballad of the Sad Café* and the fictional New England college town of *Virginia Woolf*, might easily serve as settings for a universal drama. Yet, in much of his work, particularly in the early plays, there is a suggestion, even an insistence, that the problem is a localized one, that the emptiness and loneliness of the characters are somehow the result of a collapse of values in the Western world in general, in the United States in particular. *The American Dream*, he says in his Preface to the play, is "an attack on the substitution of artificial for real values in our society." Such an attack is implicit in the depiction of Peter in *The Zoo Story*.

It is in *Virginia Woolf* that this side of Albee's "truth" is most evident. He is not content that his characters perform an action which carries implications for an audience that far transcend the action itself. He must distribute labels. George may jokingly identify himself, as history professor, with the humanities, and Nick, as biology professor, with science, and turn their meeting into a historical-inevitability parable about the necessary decline of the West, but Albee presumably means it. Calling the town New Carthage and giving George significant throwaway lines ("When I was sixteen and going to prep school, during the Punic Wars . . .") are cute ways of underlining a ponderous intention. I would not go so far as Diana Trilling (*Esquire*, December 1963) and suggest that George and Martha are the Washingtons, or Henry Hewes (*The Best Plays of 1962–1963*), that Nick is like Nikita Khrushchev, but Albee is plainly intent on giving his sterility tale an obvious cultural point. Martha's joke when Nick fails to "make it in the sack" is apparently no joke at all: "But that's how it is in a civilized society."

My own tendency is to brush all this grandiose symbol-making under the rug to protect what I admire in *Virginia Woolf*. If we can believe Albee's remarks in the *Diplomat* interview, however, all this comprises the "play's subtleties"; in faulting the movie version of his play, he says, "the entire political argument was taken out, the argument between history and science." The chasm that confronts the Albee characters may, then, be existential chaos or a materialistic society corrupt enough to make a culture hero out of . . . (whom? to each critic his own horrible example, and there are those would pick Albee himself), or a combination in which the second of these is an image of the first.

There is nothing unusual about this slightly unstable mixture of philosophic assumption and social criticism; it can be found in the work of Tennessee Williams and, from quite a different perspective, that of Eugène Ionesco. The differentiation is useful primarily because it provides us with insight into the shape that Albee gives his material. If the lost and lonely Albee character is an irrevocable fact—philosophically, theologically, psychologically—if all that *angst* is inescapable, then his plays must necessarily be reflections of that condition; any gestures of defiance are doomed to failure. If, however, the Albee character is a product of his societal context and if that context is changeable (not necessarily politically, but by an alteration

of modes of behavior between one man and another), then the plays may be
instructive fables. He has dismissed American drama of the 1930s as pro-
paganda rather than art, and he has disavowed solutions to anything. Still,
in several statements he has suggested that there are solutions—or, at least,
alternatives. Surely that possibility is implicit in his description of *The American Dream* as an "attack." In the *Transatlantic Review* interview, he said that
"the responsibility of the writer is to be a sort of demonic social critic—to
present the world and people in it as he sees it and say 'Do you like it? If
you don't like it change it.' " In the *Atlantic*, he said, "I've always thought
. . . that it was one of the responsibilities of playwrights to show people
how they are and what their time is like in the hope that perhaps they'll
change it."

Albee, then, shares with most American playwrights an idea of the
utility of art, the supposition not only that art should convey truth, but that
it should do so to some purpose. There is a strong strain of didacticism in
all his work, but it is balanced by a certain ambiguity about the nature of
the instructive fable. In interviews, he harps on how much of the creative
process is subconscious, how little he understands his own work, how a play
is to be experienced rather than understood. Insofar as this is not sour grapes
pressed to make an aesthetic (his reaction to the reviews of *Tiny Alice*), it
may be his way of recognizing that there is a conflict between his attitude
toward man's situation and his suspicion (or hope: certainly *conviction* is too
strong a word) that something can, or ought, to be done about it; between
his assumption that this is hell we live in and his longing to redecorate it.

Whatever the nature of the chasm on the edge of which the Albee
characters teeter so dexterously, to disturb the balance is to invite disaster
or—possibly—salvation. If the conflict that I suggest above is a real one, it
should be reflected in the plays in which one or more characters are willing
to risk disaster. *The American Dream* and *The Sandbox* can be passed over here
because, except for the sentimental death of Grandma at the end of the latter,
they are diagnostic portraits of the Albee world, not actions performed in
that setting. *The Death of Bessie Smith* and *The Ballad of the Sad Café* are more
to the point, but they are also special cases. Although risks are taken (the
Intern goes outside to examine Bessie; Amelia takes in Cousin Lymon in
Ballad), the plays are less concerned with these acts than they are with the
kind of expositional presentation—not particularly satirical in this case—
that we get in *Dream*. Even so, the Intern's risk is meaningless since the
woman is already dead; and Amelia's love is necessarily doomed by the
doctrine the McCullers novella expounds—that it is difficult to love but
almost impossible to be loved—and by the retrospective form the play took

when Albee saddled it with a maudlin message-giving narrator. *Tiny Alice* and *Malcolm* are two of a kind, particularly if we consider them as corruption-of-innocence plays, although there is also a similarity of sorts between Malcolm's attempt to put a face on his absent father and Julian's attempt to keep from putting a face on his abstracted Father. They are even similar in that Albee, sharing a popular-comedy misconception about what that snake was up to in the Garden, uses sex as his sign of corruption—ludicrously in *Alice*, snickeringly in *Malcolm*. Traditionally, one of two things happens in plays in which the innocent face the world: either they become corrupted and learn to live with it (the standard Broadway maturity play) or they die young and escape the corruption (Synge's *Deirdre of the Sorrows* or Maxwell Anderson's *Winterset*). In the Albee plays, both things happen. Julian dies after accepting the world (edited to fit his preconceptions about it) and Malcolm dies, muttering "I've . . . lost so much," and loss, as the plays from *The Zoo Story* to *A Delicate Balance* insist, is what you gain in learning to live with it. There are extenuating circumstances for the deaths in these plays (Julian's concept of God is tied in with his desire to be a martyr; Malcolm's death is borrowed from Purdy, although Albee does not seem to understand what Purdy was doing with it in the novel), but these plays, too, are illustrations of the Albee world, and the deaths are more sentimental than central. *Everything in the Garden* is such an unlikely wedding of Albee and the late Giles Cooper, whose English play was the source of the American adaptation, that it is only superficially characteristic of Albee's work.

It is in *The Zoo Story*, *Who's Afraid of Virginia Woolf?* and *A Delicate Balance* that one finds dramatic actions by which the ambiguity of Albee's attitudes may be tested. In *The Zoo Story*, so goes the customary reading, Jerry confronts the vegetative Peter, forces him to stand his ground, dies finally on his own knife held in Peter's hand. In that suicidal act, Jerry becomes a scapegoat who gives his own life so that Peter will be knocked out of his complacency and learn to live, or LIVE. Even Albee believes this, or he said he did in answer to a question from Arthur Gelb (*The New York Times*, February 15, 1960): "Though he dies, he passes on an awareness of life to the other character in the play." If this is true, then presumably we are to take seriously—not as a dramatic device, but for its content—Jerry's "you have to make a start somewhere" speech in which he expounds the steps-to-love doctrine, a soggy inheritance from Carson McCullers ("A Tree. A Rock. A Cloud.") and Truman Capote (*The Grass Harp*). That the start should be something a great deal less gentle than the McCullers-Capote inheritance might suggest is not suprising when we consider that violence and death became twisted life symbols during the 1950's (as all the kids said after James Dean's fatal smashup, "Boy, that's living") and, then, turned literary in the 1960's (as in Jack Richardson's *Gallows Humor* and all the motorcycle movies from *The Wild Angels* to *Scorpio Rising*).

The problem with that reading is not that it is awash with adolescent profundity, which might well annoy some of the audience, but that it seems to be working against much that is going on within the play. Although Albee prepares the audience for the killing, it has always seemed gratuitous, a melodramatic flourish. The reason may be that it tries to suggest one thing (salvation) while the logic of the play demands something else. Except for a couple of expositional lapses, Jerry is too well drawn a character—self-pitying and aggressive, self-deluding and forlorn—to become the conventional "hero" (Albee uses that word in the Gelb interview) that the positive ending demands. He may well be so aware of his separation from everyone else that he plans or improvises ("could I have planned all this? No . . . no, I couldn't have. But I think I did") his own murder in a last desperate attempt to make contact, but there is nothing in the play to indicate that he succeeds. At the end, Peter is plainly a man knocked off his balance, but there is no indication that he has fallen into "an awareness of life." In fact, the play we are watching has already been presented in miniature in the dog story, and all Jerry gained from that encounter was "solitary but free passage." "There are some things in it that I don't really understand," Albee told Gelb. One of them may be that the play itself denies the romantic ending.

Virginia Woolf is a more slippery case. Here, too, the play works against the presumably upbeat ending, but Albee may be more aware that this is happening. According to the conventions of Broadway psychology, as reflected, for instance, in a play like William Inge's *The Dark at the Top of the Stairs*, in a moment of crisis two characters come to see themselves clearly. Out of their knowledge a new maturity is born, creating an intimacy that has not existed before and a community that allows them to face their problems (if not solve them) with new courage. This was the prevailing cliché of the serious Broadway play of the 1950s, and it was still viable enough in the 1960s to take over the last act of Lorraine Hansberry's *The Sign in Sidney Brustein's Window* and turn an interesting play into a conventional one. *Virginia Woolf* uses, or is used by, this cliché.

Although the central device of the play is the quarrel between George and Martha, the plot concerns their nonexistent son. From George's "Just don't start on the bit, that's all," before Nick and Honey enter, the play builds through hints, warnings, revelations until "sonny-Jim is created and then destroyed. Snap, goes the illusion. Out of the ruins, presumably, new strength comes. The last section, which is to be played "very softly, very slowly," finds George offering new tenderness to Martha, assuring her that the time had come for the fantasy to die, forcing her—no longer maliciously—to admit that she is afraid of Virginia Woolf. It is "Time for bed," and there is nothing left for them to do but go together to face the dark at the top of the stairs. As though the rejuvenation were not clear enough from the last scene, there is the confirming testimony in Honey's tearful reiteration "I want a child" and Nick's broken attempt to sympathize, "I'd like to. . . ." Then, too, the last act is called "The Exorcism," a name that had been the working title for the play itself.

As neat as Inge, and yet there is something wrong with it. How can a relationship like that of Martha and George, built so consistently on illusion (the playing of games), be expected to have gained something from a sudden admission of truth? What confirmation is there in Nick and Honey when we remember that she is drunk and hysterical and that he is regularly embarrassed by what he is forced to watch? There are two possibilities beyond the conventional reading suggested above. The last scene between Martha and George may be another one of their games; the death of the child may not be the end of illusion but an indication that the players have to go back to GO and start again their painful trip to home. Although there are many indications that George and Martha live a circular existence, going over the same ground again and again, the development of the plot and the tone of the last scene (the use of monosyllables, for instance, instead of their customary rhetoric) seem to deny that the game is still going on. The other possibility is that the truth— as in *The Iceman Cometh*—brings not freedom but death. To believe otherwise is to accept the truth-maturity cliché as readily as one must buy the violence-life analogy to get the positive ending of *The Zoo Story*. My own suspicion is that everything that feels wrong about the end of *Virginia Woolf* arises from the fact that, like the stabbing in *Zoo*, it is a balance-tipping ending that conventional theater says is positive but the Albee material insists is negative.

In *A Delicate Balance*, the line is clearer. The titular balance is the pattern of aggression and withdrawal, accusation and guilt which Tobias and his family have constructed in order to cope with existence. Agnes suggests that Tobias's "We do what we can" might be "Our motto." When Harry and Edna invade the premises, trying to escape from the nameless fears that have attacked them, they come under the white flag of friendship. Tobias must decide whether or not to let them stay, knowing that the "disease" they carry is contagious and that infection in the household will likely upset the balance. His problem is one in metaphysical semantics, like Julian's in *Tiny Alice*, although *God* is not the word whose meaning troubles him. "Would you give friend Harry the shirt off your back, as they say?" asks Claire, before the invasion begins. "I *suppose* I would. He *is* my best friend," answers Tobias, and we hear echoes from *The American Dream*: "She's just a dreadful woman, but she *is* chairman of our woman's club, so naturally I'm terribly fond of her." *Dream's* satirical fun about the emptiness of conventional language becomes deadly serious in *Balance*, for Tobias must decide whether the meaning of *friendship* is one with substance or only surface—whether *friendship* is a human relationship implying the possibility of action and risk, or simply a label, like *marriage* or *kinship*, to be fastened to a form of accommodation. As Pearl Bailey sang in *House of Flowers*, "What is a friend for? Should a friend bolt the door?" Tobias (having failed with his cat as Jerry failed with the dog) decides to try doing more than he can; in his long, broken speech in the last act, he displays his fear, indicates that he does not want Harry and Edna around, does not even like them, "BUT BY GOD . . . YOU STAY!!" His attempt fails because Harry and Edna, having decided that they would never risk putting real meaning into *friendship*, depart, leaving a depleted Tobias to rearrange his labels. He will have the help of Agnes, of course, which—on the balance—is a great deal, for she finds the conventional words of goodbye: "well, don't be strangers." Edna, who not many lines before made the "only skin" speech, answers, "Oh, good Lord, how could we be? Our lives are . . . the same." And so they are.

Thematically, *A Delicate Balance* is Albee's most precise statement. The gesture toward change, which seemed to fit so uncomfortably at the end of *The Zoo Story* and *Virginia Woolf*, has been rendered powerless within the action of *Balance*. Not only are Albee's characters doomed to live in the worst of all possible worlds; it is the only possible world. The impulse to do something about it can end only in failure. Yet, Albee cannot leave it at that. He cannot, like Samuel Beckett, let his characters turn their meaninglessness into ritual which has a way, on stage, of reasserting the meaning of the human being. He almost does so in *Virginia Woolf*, but his suspicion that games are not enough—a failure really to recognize that games are a form of truth as much as a form of lying—leads to the doubtful exorcism. Although the *angst*-er in Albee cannot let Tobias succeed, the latent reformer cannot help but make him heroic in his lost-cause gesture. He becomes an older, wearier, emptier Jerry, with only the unresisting air to throw himself on at the end.

"Better than nothing!" says Clov in *Endgame*. "Is it possible?" Out of the fastness of his wasteland, and against his better judgment, Albee cannot keep from hoping so.

In my critical and psychological naivety, I assume—as the paragraphs above show—that Albee's plays are really about the accommodations forced on man by his condition and his society. It is impossible, however, to get through a discussion of Albee without facing up to what might be called— on the analogy of the fashionable critical term *subtext*—his sub-subject matter. That is the "masochistic-homosexual perfume" that Robert Brustein found hanging so heavily over *The Zoo Story*. It is a perfume of little importance except insofar as it throws the audience off the scent of the play's real quarry.

A student stopped me on campus a few years ago, hoping I would be able to confirm the story that *Who's Afraid of Virginia Woolf?* was first performed by four men in a little theater in Montreal. When I expressed my doubt, he went off to call a friend in New York who knew someone who knew the man who had been stage manager . . . although somehow he never got the confirmation he wanted. Except for the circumstantiality of this account (why Montreal?), it was a familiar rumor. Albee, in the *Diplomat* interview, explained that it was a letter to the *Times* that started the whole thing, that from there it passed into print elsewhere, first as rumor, then as fact. "I know the difference between men and women," he said, "and I write both characters." The more sophisticated interpreters simply step over Albee's denials and assume that the play, whoever it was written for, is really about a homosexual marriage. The reasoning here is that homosexual marriages, lacking the sanctions of society, are extremely unstable and that to survive at all they must create fantasy devices to bind the couple together. Hence, the imaginary child—for what other kind of child could come from the union of two men? There is a kind of specious logic in operation here. The flaw in it, however, is the refusal to recognize how much fantasy is a part of any relationship, how two people who are close (husband and wife, lovers of whatever sex, good friends) invent private languages, private rituals, private games which set them off from the others. Jimmy and Alison play at squirrels-and-bears in John Osborne's *Look Back in Anger*, and Sid and Iris play wild-mountain-girl in *The Sign in Sidney Brustein's Window* without either couple being taken as surrogate homosexual unions. My own inclination would be to let Martha and George have their "little bugger," as they call the nonexistent child, without insisting that they have a big one.

I have heard the play praised for the clarity with which it presented a homosexual couple, but, for the most part, such readings are based on a rejection of the possibility that George and Martha may have a representative heterosexual marriage. A similar rejection takes place when the play is dismissed as a kind of homosexual denigration of conventional marriage. Surely the castrating female and the dominated male are such commonplace psychological stereotypes—on and off stage—that their appearance need not be taken as an indication of a perverse attempt to do in all the Darbys and Joans who provide America's divorce statistics. Besides, Martha and George do not really fit those stereotypes. They appear to at the beginning, but as the play goes on it becomes clear that they are really very evenly matched in a battle that has been going on seriously since Strindberg's *The Dance of Death* and comically since *The Taming of the Shrew*. Albee's male wins, as in Shakespeare, but only tentatively, as in Strindberg. Not that Albee is particularly interested in the battle of the sexes as such. He has his own use for it, which is not to attack heterosexuality, but to present one of his many accommodation images: a well-matched pair of antagonists form a balance of sorts.

If a play like *Virginia Woolf* could call up the homosexual echoes, it is not surprising that *Tiny Alice* set them roaring. The opening scene between Cardinal and Lawyer is an exercise in bitchiness, primly nasty and insinuating, a marked contrast to the verbal exchanges between Martha and George. It passes from Lawyer's sneering comment on the caged cardinals ("uh, together . . . in conversation, as it were") to a variation on the old joke about the suitability of a boy or a clean old man, to hints of a schoolboy affair between the two men (Lawyer: "I'll have you do your obeisances. As you used to, old friend"), to mutual accusations in which Lawyer becomes an anus-entering hyena and Cardinal a mating bird. The business of the scene is apparently expositional, setting up the donation that will send Julian to Alice, to the tension between the two characters and the implication of their past relationship is gratuitous. So, too, is Lawyer's calling Butler "Darling" and "Dearest." The homosexual overtones in Julian (his attraction to the Welsh stableman, his kissing Miss Alice's hand "as he would kiss a Cardinal's ring," and the sensuality of his martyrdom dream in which the lion seems to mount him and he lingers over the entrance of the gladiator's prongs) might be more legitimate, a suggestion of the ambiguity of celibacy. Still, since he is sacrificed to heterosexuality—in that ludicrous scene in which he buries his head in Miss Alice's crotch, a cunninlingual first for the American stage—there is justice in Philip Roth's celebrated attack on "The Play that Dare Not Speak Its Name" (*New York Review of Books*, February 25, 1965). Roth accused Albee of writing "a homosexual daydream" about the martyrdom of the celibate male and disguising it as a metaphysical drama. Several weeks later (April 8, 1965), a letter to the editor insisted that there was no disguise at all in the play because a "tiny alice" is homosexual jargon for, as the writer so coyly put it, "a masculine derrière." Acting on this information, Bernard F. Dukore added an ingenious footnote to an article in *Drama Survey* (Spring 1966) in which he considered that Julian, Butler, and Lawyer, all lovers of Miss Alice, might really be lovers of "tiny alice" and the opening doors at the end an anus symbol, but—as he went on to complain—a play that depends on a special argot for its symbolism is lost on a general audience. If "tiny alice" really is a gay word for anus and if Albee is using it consciously, he may be making an inside joke which has some relevance to his presumed serious play. If one of the points of the play is that all concepts of God (from Julian's abstraction to the mouse in the model) are creations of the men who hold them, a sardonic joke about God as a "tiny alice" is possible. Certainly, Albee has made that joke before, casually in *Virginia Woolf* (where George speaks of "Christ and all those girls") and more seriously in *The Zoo Story* (where one of the suggestions in Jerry's where-to-begin-to-love speech is "WITH GOD WHO IS A COLORED QUEEN WHO WEARS A KIMONO AND PLUCKS HIS EYEBROWS . . ."). On the other hand, the phrase could turn the play into an audience put-down such as the one described by Clay in *Dutchman*, in which he says that Bessie Smith, whatever the audience thought she was doing, was always saying, "Kiss my black ass."

This kind of speculation, hedged in as it is by *ifs* and *maybes*, is finally pointless. I almost wrote *fruitless*, but I stopped myself, assuming that my use of "inside joke" earlier is contribution enough to a silly game. How cute can a critic get without his tone corrupting his purpose? This question has relevance for the playwright, too. The problem about *Tiny Alice* is not whether there is a hidden homosexual joke and/or message, but that the obvious homosexual allusions seem to have little relevance to the plot device (the conspiracy to catch Julian), the play's central action (the martyrdom of Julian), or its presumed subject matter (the old illusion-reality problem). Unless Roth is right, the homosexual material is only decoration, different in quantity but not in kind from the additions and emphases that Albee brought to the already campy (old style) surface of Purdy's *Malcolm*.

The Zoo Story is the only Albee play in which a homosexual reading seems possible and usable in terms of what else the play is doing. It is, after all, the account of a meeting between two men in Central Park ("I'm not the gentleman you were expecting," says Jerry), in which one lets himself be impaled by the other, who has a phallic name. Jerry, dying, says, "I came unto you (*He laughs, so faintly*) and you have comforted me. Dear Peter." Jerry's casual references to the "colored queen" and the police "chasing fairies down from trees" on the other side of the park; his story of his one real love affair with the park superintendent's son, whom Otto Reinert (in *Modern Drama*) identifies with Peter by virtue of Peter's "proprietary claim" to the park bench; the implications in Jerry's "with fury because the pretty little ladies aren't pretty little ladies, with making money with your body which is an act of love and I could prove it"—all contribute to the possibility of this being a homosexual encounter. If it is, then much of the verbal and physical business of the play—Jerry's teasing, his wheedling, his tickling, the wrestling struggle for the bench—can be seen as an elaborate seduction which, since Jerry forces his partner to hold the knife, can only be summed up as getting a rise out of Peter. The dramatic fable can be read this way and still be relevant to the thematic material discussed earlier in this chapter. The problem comes when we consider the end of the play. If it is the positive ending that Albee suggested in the Gelb interview, if Jerry has passed on his "awareness of life," it must be Peter's initiation, and that, as Jerry says earlier, is "jazz of a very special hotel." On the other hand, as John Rechy keeps insisting in his seemingly endless novel, *City of Night*, a homosexual pickup in a park is a particularly workable image for the failure of contact between people.

"You know, I almost think you're serious," says Nick about something other than drama criticism, and George answers, "No, baby . . . *you* almost think you're serious, and it scares the hell out of you."

I feel a little that way about my very plausible reading of *The Zoo Story* in the section above. For if I am willing to accept the possibility of Peter as phallus, how can I deny all the interpreters who insist on seeing Jerry as Christ and Peter as the rock upon which to build his church? At least, the analogy of the homosexual pickup works comfortably within the action of the play and, less comfortably, with the thematic material. Despite the Biblical echoes ("I came unto you" again), the Christ-Jerry analogue is possible only to the extent that every sacrificial victim is a Christ figure, but that is a tautology which contributes nothing to an understanding of the play. If we see Jerry's suicidal finish as a sacrifice, we learn precious little about his action by nodding wisely and saying: oh, ho, Christ. We might as well say: oh, ho, Sydney Carton. Still, writers will use mythic and historical identifications for their characters (Tennessee Williams in *Orpheus Descending*), and critics will go myth-hunting and trap the slippery beasts. It has now become customary to dive into the underbrush of each new Albee play and bring them back alive.

Albee is partly to blame. He uses obvious symbols such as the muscular young man who is *The American Dream* and the athletic death figure in *The Sandbox*. He asks Julian and Miss Alice to form a pietà in *Tiny Alice* and the dying Julian to spread his arms to "resemble a crucifixion." In some notes prepared for a press conference, later printed in *The Best Plays of 1964–1965*, Albee said of *Tiny Alice:* "The play is full of symbols and allusions, naturally, but they are to be taken as echoes in a cave, things overheard, not fully understood at first." I take this to mean that they have no functional use in the play, in relation to either character or action, and that at best they provide a texture as allusive words do in some poetry. In a play, as in a poem, an allusion may uncover another realm of possibility (for instance, the ironies that keep emerging in *Peer Gynt*), but it can do so only if it does not wreck itself on the dramatic facts of the play. Take that pietà, for instance. It must either make clear something in the relationship between Julian and Miss Alice that has been implicit all along, or it must seem—as it did on stage— an exercise in literary pretentiousness.

Tiny Alice is the most blatant, but all the Albee plays insist on suggesting that there is more there than meets the eye and ear. This can be seen in the way Albee appears to be playing with the significance-seekers. In Agnes's "We become allegorical, my darling Tobias, as we grow older." In George's "Well, it's an allegory, really—probably—but it can be read as straight, cozy prose." Of course, Albee may mean this, too. In either case, he deserves to have the significant-name game played in his dramatic front yard. So Jerry becomes not only Christ but Jeremiah, and Julian not only Christ but Julian the Apostate. The Washingtons and the Khrushchevs get into *Virginia Woolf*. When Agnes, commenting on how much Claire has seen, says, "You were not named for nothing," she is presumably making a nasty crack about *claire* as an adjective meaning *bright*. Yet audiences came out of the theater asking questions about St. Clare, St. Agnes, the Apocryphal Tobias, and even Miss Julie.

Albee may be fond of symbols and allusions, echoes and things over-heard, but he plainly does not work—as the search for mythic analogies suggests—with dramatic images that come from outside his plays. This does not mean that he is the naturalist he occasionally claims to be, as when he told a *New York Times* interviewer (September 18, 1966) that even *Tiny Alice* was naturalistic. Even in *Virginia Woolf*, which is certainly the most natu-ralistic of his plays, the situation is basically unrealistic; the drinking party is a revelatory occasion, not a slice of life in a small New England college. For the most part, his characters have neither setting nor profession, and when they are defined by things, the process is either conventionally (Peter's possessions) or unconventionally (the contents of Jerry's room) stereotypical, so obviously so that realism is clearly not intended. Nor do the characters have biographies, at least of the kind one has come to expect from the psychological naturalism of the Broadway stage. *Virginia Woolf*, harping as it does on the parental hang-ups of its two principals, comes closest to that pattern, but it is never very clear in this play how much of the memory is invention, which of the facts are fantasy. If *Virginia Woolf* and *The Zoo Story*

are, at most, distant cousins of naturalistic drama, how much more remote
are Albee's plainly absurdist plays (*The Sandbox, The American Dream*), his
"mystery" play with its label-bearing characters (*Tiny Alice*), his drawing-
room noncomedy (*A Delicate Balance*).

A close look at Albee's language provides the clearest indication of the
nonrealistic character of his plays. *A Delicate Balance* is the most obvious
example. The lines are consciously stilted, broken by elaborate parenthesis
("It follows, to my mind, that since I speculate I might, some day, or early
evening I think more likely—some autumn dusk—go quite mad") or pulled
up short by formal negative endings ("Must she not?"; "is it not?")—devices
that call for inflections which stop the natural flow of speech. There are lines
that are barely comprehensible ("One does not apologize to those for whom
one must?"), which cannot be read without great deliberation. The verbal
elaboration has particular point in this play since the langauge itself becomes
a reflection of the artificiality of the characters and the setting, a pattern in
which form replaces substance. This can best be seen in the play's most
intricate digression. "What I find most astonishing," Agnes begins as the
play opens, only to interrupt herself with her fantasy on madness. Her
thought meanders through Tobias's practical attempt to get the after-dinner
drinks, and we are fifteen speeches into the play, past two reappearances of
the "astonish" phrase, before her opening sentence finally comes to an end.
Seems to end, really, for the phrase recurs just before the final curtain, as
Agnes goes her placidly relentless way—"to fill a silence," as the stage direction says—as though the intrusion of Harry and Edna and Tobias's painful
attempt to deal with it were an easily forgotten interruption of the steady
flow of nonevent.

In the *Atlantic* interview, explaining why he felt that English actors
were needed for *Tiny Alice*, Albee said that he had moved from the "idiomatic"
language of *Virginia Woolf* to something more formal. *A Delicate Balance* is a
further step in elaboration. Yet, the language of the earlier plays, however
idiomatic, is plainly artificial. Albee has used three main verbal devices from
the beginning: interruption, repetition, and the set speech, the last of which
makes use of the first two. The set speeches are almost formal recitations,
as the playwright recognizes in *The Zoo Story* when he lets Jerry give his
monologue a title: "THE STORY OF JERRY AND THE DOG!" There
are similar speeches in all the plays: Jack's "Hey . . . Bessie" monologue
which is the whole of scene 3 of *Bessie Smith*; the Young Man's sentimental
mutilation speech in *The American Dream*; George's "bergin" story and Martha's "Abandon-ed" speech in *Virginia Woolf*; the narrator's speeches in *Ballad*;
Julian's dying soliloquy in *Tiny Alice*; Madame Girard's Entre-Scene mono-

logue in *Malcolm;* Jack's direct address to the audience in *Garden*. Although Albee does not direct the speaker to step into a spotlight—as Tennessee Williams does with comparable speeches in *Sweet Bird of Youth*—he recognizes that these are essentially solo performances even when another character is on stage to gesture or grunt or single-word his way into the uneven but persistent flow of words. Of Tobias's big scene at the end of *Balance*, Albee says "This next is an aria." In *The Zoo Story*, Jerry does not use a simple narration; his story is momentarily stopped for generalizing comments ("It always happens when I try to simplify things; people look up. But that's neither hither nor thither") and marked with repeated words ("The dog is black, all black; all black except . . .") and phrases ("I'll kill the dog with kindness, and if that doesn't work . . . I'll just kill him"). The word *laughter* punctuates the "bergin" story the way laughter itself presumably broke the cocktail-lounge murmur of the bar in which the boys were drinking.

It is not the long speeches alone that are built of interruption and repetition; that is the pattern of all the dialogue. On almost any page of *Virginia Woolf* you can find examples as obvious as this speech of George's: "Back when I was courting Martha—well, don't know if that's exactly the right word for it—but back when I was courting Martha. . . ." Then comes Martha's "Screw, sweetie!" followed by another attempt from George, more successful this time, "At any rate, back when I was courting Martha," and off he goes into an account which involves their going "into a bar . . . you know, a *bar* . . . a whiskey, beer, and bourbon *bar*. . . ." Sometimes the repetitions become echoes that reach from act to act as when Martha's "snap" speech in Act Two is picked up by George in the snapdragon scene in Act Three. From *The Zoo Story* to *Everything in the Garden*, then, Albee has consciously manipulated language for effect; even when it sounds most like real speech—as in *Virginia Woolf*—it is an exercise in idiomatic artificiality.

At their best, these artifices are the chief devices by which Albee presents his dramatic images. Neither naturalist nor allegorist, he works the great middle area where most playwrights operate. He puts an action on stage— an encounter in a park that becomes a suicide-murder, a night-long quarrel that ends in the death of illusion, an invasion that collapses before the defenders can decide whether to surrender or to fight—which presumably has dramatic vitality in its own right and from which a meaning or meanings can emerge. The central situation—the encounter, the relationship implicit in the quarrel, the state of the defenders and the invaders—is defined almost completely in verbal terms. There is business of course, but it is secondary. Jerry's poking and tickling Peter is only an extension of what he has been doing with words; George's attempt to strangle Martha is a charade not far removed from their word games. When events get more flamboyant—the shooting of Julian, Julia's hysterical scene with the gun—they tend to become ludicrous. The most obvious example in Albee of physical business gone wrong is the wrestling match between Miss Amelia and Marvin Macy in *The Ballad of the Sad Café*; the fact that it is the dramatic climax of the play does not keep it from looking silly on stage. Ordinarily, Albee does not need to ask his characters to *do* very much, for what they *say* is dramatic action. "The old pigeonhole bit?" says Jerry in *The Zoo Story*, and although it is he, not Peter, who does the pigeonholing, the accusation and the mockery in the question is an act of aggression, as good as a shove for throwing Peter off balance.

In the long run, Albee's reputation as a playwright will probably depend less on what he has to say than on the dramatic situations through which he says it. The two Albee plays that seem to have taken the strongest hold on the public imagination (which may be a way of saying they are the two plays I most admire) are *The Zoo Story* and *Virginia Woolf*. The reason is that the meeting between Jerry and Peter and the marriage of George and Martha, for all the nuances in the two relationships, are presented concretely in gesture and line; they take shape on the stage with great clarity. *Tiny Alice*, by contrast, is all amorphousness. It may finally be possible to reduce that play to an intellectual formulation, but the portentousness that hovers over so many lines and so much of the business keeps the characters and the situation from attaining dramatic validity. *The Zoo Story* is more successful as a play, not because its dramatic situation is more realistic, but because it exists on stage—a self-created dramatic fact.

A Delicate Balance is a much stronger play than *Tiny Alice*. As the discussion early in this chapter indicates, it is probably Albee's most perfect combination of theme and action, and its central metaphor—the balance— is important not only to the play but to Albee's work as a whole. Yet, compared to *Virginia Woolf*, it is an incredibly lifeless play. The reason, I think, is that the Martha-George relationship has dramatic substance in a way that the Tobias-Agnes household does not. Too much has been made— particularly by casual reviewers—of the violence, the hate, the anger in the Martha-George marriage. It is just as important that the quarrel be seen in the context of the affection they have for one another and the life—even if it is a long, sad game—which they so obviously share. One of the best inventions in all of Albee is the gun with the parasol in it, for what better way of seeing the relationship of Martha and George than in terms of a murderous weapon that is also a sheltering object; the instrument is a metaphor for the marriage, and its use is a preview of what will happen in the last act.

From the moment the play opens, from Martha's challenge, "What a dump. Hey what's that from?" it is clear that Martha and George play the same games. He may be tired at first, not really in the mood for a session of name-the-movie, or he may be faking indifference because he cannot remember that the "goddamn Bette Davis picture" Martha has in mind is *Beyond the Forest* (1949), but there is companionship in the incipient quarrel that will not disappear as the argument grows more lethal. It can be seen directly in several places. Near the beginning of the play, after a mutual accusation of baldness, they go into a momentary affectionate scene in which his "Hello honey" leads to her request for "big sloppy kiss." Almost the same phrase, "C'mon . . . give me a kiss," is her compliment for his having been clever enough to introduce the parasol-gun into the game room. Much more important than the grand games to which he gives labels—Humiliate the Host, Get the Guests, Hump the Hostess—are the small games that they play constantly—the play-acting routines, the little-kid bits, the mock-etiquette turns, the verbal games. The whole force of the play depends on their existence as a couple, a relationship made vivid in moments such as the one in act 3 when Nick, humiliated at his sexual failure, begins angrily, "I'm nobody's houseboy . . ." and Martha and George shout in unison, "Now!" and then begin to sing, "I'm nobody's houseboy now. . . ." Their closeness is important if we are to recognize that George can be and is cuckolded. This event takes place on stage in act 2 when Martha and Nick dance together sensuously and, speaking in time to the music, she tells about George's abortive attempt to be a novelist. It is at this moment that their marriage is violated, that George's anger shows most plainly, that he initiates a game of Get the Guests. "Book dropper! Child mentioner!" accuses George, and we see—perhaps before he does—the connection that forces him to carry "the bit about the kid" to its murderous conclusion. One may come away from *Virginia Woolf* suspicious of the end of the play and its presumed implications but never in doubt about the dramatic force of either characters or situation.

A Delicate Balance provides a marked contrast. We learn a great deal about the antipathy between Agnes and Claire, the sexual life of Agnes and Tobias, the marriage problems of Julia, the nameless fears of Edna and Harry, but the situation is explained more than it is presented. Some of the language is witty, some of it—particularly Agnes's lines—is quietly bitchy, but speeches do not pass from one character to another, carving out a definition of their relationship; lines fall from the mouths of the characters and shatter on the stage at their feet. Thematically, this is fine, since separateness is what Albee wants to depict, and he is ingenious in the way he lets the artificiality of his language contribute to the general sense of empty façade.

Unfortunately, the characters are defined only in terms of their separateness, their significance as exemplary lost ones. Not so indeterminate as *Tiny Alice*, *A Delicate Balance* still lacks the kind of concreteness that comes from a dramatic image fully realized on stage. The characters are given a little biography, a few mannerisms, a whisper of depth, but they remain highly articulate stick figures moving through a sequence of nonevents to a foregone conclusion.

Unless Edward Albee is on some unannounced road to Damascus, there is not much doubt about what he will be saying in the plays that lie ahead of him. It is how he chooses to say it that will be important. In the face of his most recent work, in which significance seems to be imposed from the outside instead of meaning rising from within, we have every reason to be afraid, not of, but for *Virginia Woolf*.

PAUL WITHERINGTON

Albee's Gothic: The Resonances of Cliché

The clear popular success of *Tiny Alice* and the smoke raised by critical analyses of that play constitute extremes that exaggerate the Albee situation, but illuminate, in doing so, our mixed reaction to the other plays. The choice of attitudes toward *Tiny Alice* seems limited at times to that of the thrilled audiences in New York, San Francisco, and London, or that of tedious scholarly legerdemain. Or the cloud of contempt: Susan Sontag writes of Albee's "sensationalism masking as cultural exposé," and Martin Gottfried writes of the play's "drowning in holy water over its head." But Gottfried goes on to admit the dramatic power of *Tiny Alice*, and an earlier comment on the play's limitations suggests a solution to his divided reaction and to our dilemma: "His [Albee's] discussion of philosophical material is hampered by a weakness of vocabulary, a propensity for exaggeration and an interest in the popular rather than the classical."

Gottfried assumes an Albee trying unsuccessfully to write like Yeats, or even Arthur Miller. But suppose we take Albee at his word—in his preface that denies the need for a preface—that *Tiny Alice* is "quite clear." Then we can start from a position that Albee's restricted vocabulary, exaggeration, and popularization are deliberate, and that what most audiences sense in the play has somehow evaded most critics. We are led in *Tiny Alice* and in all of Albee's plays to consider a popular form and language with great theatrical power and yet confusing anti-intellectual undercurrents. That form and language are those of modern Gothic literature, and they are the factors

From *Comparative Drama* (1970). © 1970 by *Comparative Drama*.

behind our mixed reaction. For the Gothic, like Frankenstein's monster, has always suffered from being overly popular and critically misinterpreted.

That Gothic is a concept broader than the melodramatic chase and ravishment novels of the late eighteenth century has been amply demonstrated by Leslie Fiedler and Irving Malin who have traced its Americanization in the nineteenth and twentieth centuries, and its endurance as a popular form can be verified by visiting the collection of contemporary Gothic paperbacks in almost any bookstore. Devendra P. Varma's *The Gothic Flame* is an eloquent plea for readmitting the traditional Gothic to scholarly consideration, and although he does not deal with modern Amercan works, his definition of Gothic allows us to cross the gap not only between traditional and modern, but between serious and popular.

Traditional Gothic, as Varma describes it, was a revolt against the Age of Reason, against the decline of religion and the increase of materialism. It celebrated "the beckoning shadows of a more intimate and mystical interpretation of life." On the one hand, Gothic restored a sense of the numinous, and on the other it correlated strongly with the emotional expressions of a revolutionary scene, linking "the Terrors of the French Revolution and the Novel of Terror in England." Varma might be describing the modern mood with its reactions against the "establishment," its almost paradoxical insistence on inner experience and outer involvement, and above all the linkings of cults of religious experience and cults of terror, as during the Inquisition— the rise of pop Satanism and the do-it-yourself bomb.

The setting, action, and imagery of contemporary Gothic reveal that it may be described as a reactionary form arising when social institutions are in a process of decline, but when the feeling of individual possibilities is in ferment through the rediscovery of mysterious forces within. The fact that Gothic is generated in the shadow of society's ruins may explain the clichéd forms and language that appall many literary critics.

If there are structural similarities between myth and metaphor, as Howard Nemerov recently notes, one can posit a similar relationship between the clichés of Gothic forms and language. Cliché of form or language appears to be a defensive and even deterministic residue—myth or metaphor stripped of its possibilities and rendered somewhat paranoic. Gothic forms, often haunted by werewolves and vampires—that is, the "undead—are the narrative equivalent of verbal cliché, language that cannot fully live or die. Both are scorned as communication on an intellectual level but refuse to die on a popular level, providing endless embarrassment to their critics.

Critics have not always taken the time to distinguish between works with clichés in them and clichéd works. In modern Gothic, cliché is often not just a satiric attack on the institutionalization and abstraction of human relationship, but through imaginative new contexts a means to transcendence of the ordinary, restricted world. Albee's works develop the richness in cliché, the magic of its buried potential. As Marshall McLuhan says of a Stanley Spencer painting, the technique involved is that of much popular art, "evoking ritual from the routine," or summoning "the archetypal from the cliché."

Three aspects of the Gothic may be distinguished in Albee's plays: reduction, inversion, and recognition. In traditional Gothic works these would most likely function in the order given to show, in a definite hero movement toward enlightenment and transcendence, a process similar to that of the archetypal quest. Reduction is a deliberate narrowing of purpose and perception to obtain concentration and direction, inversion is a confused maze of trial and initiation, and recognition is a conquering or assimilating of alien forces or identities. Although these aspects occur clearly in Albee, the movement between them is not always certain. There is no straightforward Gothic plot and no clear-cut Gothic hero, with the possible exception of Julian in *Tiny Alice*. Moreover, as one would expect in a writer who owes so much to the Theater of the Absurd, enlightenment or transcendence is always severely limited.

Finally, as we pursue the Gothic in Albee, it will be clear that he is a major satirist, and that the Gothic does not diminish that stance; both schools, after all, have traditionally attacked the institutions of authority and the irrationality of what passes for reason. Albee's genius lies in the balance he achieves between satire's pessimistic cycle and Gothic possibilities for transcendence that are inherent in the grimmest horror.

Reduction is a standard Gothic device employed to create suspense or to heighten drama. As Irving Malin points out, the Gothic world is a microcosm, intensive rather than extensive. Hence the emphasis on family, isolated castle or abbey, and the hidden garden or room. Reduction allows an emphasis on subjective states of mind. According to Varma, the eighteenth-century Gothic novel pioneered in "spotlighting individual scenes," a dramatic method which led in turn to the psychological novel. The theater is a natural location for Gothic, but ironically we may fail to recognize many Gothic dramas because the claptrap we traditionally associate with Gothic— mists, flying bats, and bloody wounds—are not usually rendered on the stage. We look for the frills and overlook the essence.

Sometimes the reductive aspect seems overly defensive, a retreat from life, as Thoreau's experiment at Walden or any modern hippie commune seems to the uninitiated. From this point of view Albee is satirizing the limitations of the American experience, or absurd defensive gestures. The bench of *The Zoo Story* emphasizes Peter's stolidarity, his typically American concept of freedom as spatial, and his fear of Jerry's circling irrationality. Likewise, the Admissions Desk in *The Death of Bessie Smith* which Nurse refuses to leave, the boxes in *The American Dream*, the bathroom (offstage) in *Who's Afraid of Virginia Woolf?* where Honey lies on the floor and peels labels, the daughter's room in *A Delicate Balance* (also offstage) which is usurped by the frightened guests, and the box that is both setting and chorus for Albee's recent *Box* and *Quotations from Chairman Mao Tse-Tung*—all serve as sanctuaries and symbols of incomplete responses to life.

The form of retreat is often a square enclosure—a room, a box, or a four-cornered relationship like that in *Who's Afraid of Virginia Woolf?*, *Tiny Alice*, or *A Delicate Balance* where reduction is guarded by a sort of closed, circular inertia. The characters in *A Delicate Balance* love in a circular sequence, as Claire points out to Tobias: "You love Agnes and Agnes loves Julia and Julia loves me and I love you." Similarly in *Who's Afraid of Virginia Woolf?*, George's Spenglerian view of the cycles of history, echoed in his remark to Nick, "Good, better, best, bested," forms a defense against Nick's linear attack on chromosomes. The four characters of *Box* and *Quotations from Chairman Mao Tse-Tung* do not appear to be aware of each other, but their speeches function in counterpoint, a musical square linking their individual retreats from complexity.

Reduction also operates through the clichés of language. The saturation of "going to do" and "going to go" in *The Death of Bessie Smith* becomes a defense against actual movement or commitment. The characters hide behind labels: Nurse is "on admissions," and Intern—his name suggesting a narcissistic reduction—is "on emergencies." Like the Mommies and Daddies of *The Sandbox* and *The American Dream*, or Butler, Lawyer, and Cardinal of *Tiny Alice*, or Old Woman of *Box* and *Quotations from Chairman Mao Tse-Tung* who recites over and over the trite words to "Over the Hill to the Poor-House," or Mao himself whose party line is heavily clichéd, they have tagged their lives with safetied roles.

In *A Delicate Balance* Tobias, like George in the earlier play, makes "neat, snappy phrases." But the real control is in Agnes's language, the exaggerated preciseness of which points to her inner insecurity. She is a nanny, a drill sergeant (Julia complains) to the other characters, more concerned with surfaces than with realities. To her sister she says, with only the least bit of humor, "If you want to kill yourself—then do it *right!*" Her control keeps the lid on the other characters' regressive fantasies: Claire's topless bathing suit, Tobias's island, and Julia's periodic return home. Examine Agnes's first speech, a single rigidly controlled sentence which struggles over several pages of qualifications and parenthetical remarks until it reaches its point.

But some of Albee's characters transcend their clichéd situation or language to the degree that they are in control of it. George and Martha's "exercising" is really a highly controlled plan (and perhaps pun) leading to the eventual "exorcising" of cliché, as later sections will show. The plans are not always so extreme, but several of the characters in the other plays direct their own reduction, even their own martyrdom. And herein lies the possibility for expansion that occurs in all the plays, what Lee Baxandall has called "some characters' imaginative power to force events, not toward historically viable solutions, but at least into channels which are telling and satisfying symbolically."

For Gothic writers, reduction of life or thought to what Thoreau calls "its lowest terms" is never merely an intellectual game as it was for him or for Descartes, neither of whom ever seriously doubted his conclusions. Gothic writers treat reduction as a certain horror from which escape is uncertain. The hero half jumps, half falls into this state, and his growth of awareness does not necessarily depend upon an unclouded will. Doubt is not a method but a condition, and delivery from crisis is a magic that must be earned. As Alice in Wonderland realizes in her own reduced state, there is always the possibility of drowning in one's own tears.

In both *The Sandbox* and *The American Dream*, Grandma is cast as a kind of director who emerges to bring individuality out of a world of stereotypes. The sandbox, for all its incongruity, is the only "real" setting in that play, just as Grandma is the only rounded character. And in *The American Dream* we feel that whatever is worthwhile leaves with Grandma in her boxes which seem to function as symbolic wombs of the imagination. The box in Albee's latest play is also a womb of imagination, for although he uses it to symbolize what is square and spiritless in our culture (and perhaps in our modern theater) and suggests that it is an example of the decline of art into craft, he says the box is solid and roomy, the example of how crafts "have come up . . . if not to replace, then . . . occupy." The box is a result of what happens "when art begins to hurt" by reminding us of the unattainable. Like the Gothic, perhaps, the box reflects the ambiguities of the modern age and the compromise with idealism that appears in the popularization of art.

Jerry's magic in *The Zoo Story* consists of restricting Peter's space in order to force his reaction along a scale from vegetable apathy to the animal passion of love or hate to the complex human reaction of love *and* hate, to an interplay of sympathy wherein attack and defense, cruelty and kindness, and murder and suicide become one. Thus individuality is achieved paradoxically through sacrifice of the self to the other, Jerry of his life and Peter of his innocence.

A similar restriction of space occurs in *Who's Afraid of Virginia Woolf?* Mike Nichols, conscious of his difficulty in transferring the play to film, has spoken of trying to preserve "the essential claustrophobic quality of the play." It is important to note that the magic brought about by inversion and recognition is based on this controlled claustrophobia, a feat of spatial limitation like that of a modern encounter group, directed by George and Martha.

Direction takes a different turn in *Tiny Alice* as Julian is martyred to the other characters. Intending to direct his reduction into the model, they in fact reveal their own reduced states. The lawyer's narrowness with words (he corrects Julian and Butler when they misuse terms) signifies his retreat from the complexities of poetry which he once wrote, according to one of his teachers, with "all the grace of a walking crow." Like Agnes he maintains control of others and of himself by the angularity of his rhetoric, as his ritually repeated remark indicates after he has shot Julian: "All legal, all accomplished, all satisfied, that which we believe." His profession is his retreat as it is for Cardinal whose situation of duplicity is emblemized by the two cardinals in a cage in his garden, or for Butler who tends to the sealed dust-free model, or the professional spinster Miss Alice who fixes herself in every room with a private chair: "One needs the feel of specific possession in every . . . area." Their use of "we"—every character except Julian adopts a professional plural—is their defense against the vulnerability of the human personality. They have made of the model a doll's house where God, if he exists, lives as a mouse, insulated from their world as they are insulated from the larger macrocosm outside their house. As Miss Alice says, one must "reduce or enlarge to . . . to what we can understand." Julian demonstrates that this, too, is an oversimplification by his final acceptance of reduction *as* enlargement, the transcending paradox that turns their fulfillment into his fulfillment.

Inversion is a traditional Gothic device to show the confusion resulting when man misuses power or probes beyond his limit. It is a logical consequence of reduction, of things brought so close that their ordinary structure collapses to the eye or mind. In the early novels of Horace Walpole and Matthew Lewis Gregory portraits or statues cry or bleed, objects reach out from a psychic universe, and life and death become uncertain categories. Inversion also occurs within the confused labyrinth of the castle where secret panels and trapdoors snare the innocent and events are contrived to blur the edges of dream and reality. In the maze, confusion may be a dead end, may lead to further defensive reduction, but it may be the prelude to a spiritual turnabout, to the liberation of the ego through a recognition that shocks one, as does the therapeutic edge of satire, into new dimensions of thought. But whereas satire and the absurd often enlighten the audience at the cost of the characters' continuing ignorance, the Gothic develops character to its highest degree of awareness.

Albee dramatizes inversion as a breakthrough of the extraordinary into the everyday routine, a process similar to the rape or seduction of innocence in older Gothic novels. In *The Death of Bessie Smith*, the real emergency of Bessie's dying tests the sterile routine of the hospital. Peter in *The Zoo Story* and Julian in *Tiny Alice* are tested when their comfortable ways of life are questioned and finally forced to the breaking point by the unconventional story of Jerry in the one play and the strange request of the four schemers in the other play.

The well-ordered world of the Long-Winded Lady in *Box* and *Quotations from Chairman Mao Tse-Tung* collapses when she falls off the ship—"The one thing you do *not* do is fall off the ship"—and is forced in aftermath of this to review the death of her husband, not the death itself, a logical end, but the messiness of the dying from cancer, "long, and coarse, and ugly, and cruel." The sloppiness of life and death she has discovered has led her to the "box," searching like Agnes for the right word to define her experience and the rationalization that will restore her balance.

In *A Delicate Balance* uninvited guests test a family relationship, whether it will survive the unlikely but perfectly logical demands that friends make on "one of those days when everything's underneath." Tobias and Agnes fail the test, not because the invasion is so strange but because the invaders are so familiar. The recognition in *A Delicate Balance* is more subtle than that of the other plays where unusual characters or events or illusions are stressed, for it argues that in time one's very mediocrity may come to life and demand an accounting. Here, as in the other plays, intrusion upon routine is not only a cause of the play's crisis but in a sense the effect of the real crisis existing at the play's start, the defensive gestures that ironically render one defenseless, like the innocent Gothic heroine who locks her doors against the horror and finds it waiting inside.

Albee's plays celebrate age rather than youth, deliberately inverting contemporary American values. Albee suggests that inversion as a true test comes only in middle years where the sense of the ordinary is strongest, and that youth itself is often an over-simplification. The youth-age conflict is sharpest in *The Sandbox* and *The American Dream* where Grandma is forced in one instance to bury herself in sand and in the other to dodder in a corner until the van men come for her. But Grandma steals the show (literally in *The American Dream* as objects in the home begin to disappear into her boxes), dominating the action and providing the only viable point of view. The generation gap occurs also in *Who's Afraid of Virginia Woolf?* and *A Delicate Balance*, and in each case age comes out ahead. George and Martha shatter the confidence of Nick and Honey by refusing to give up Berlin. George's metaphor for the possibilities, the creative illusions of life. In the later play Julia learns the complexities of human interaction from her wiser parents and still wiser aunt, Claire. Each play begins by appearing to discredit age and ends by endowing it with a kind of saving power. When youth avoids its responsibilities or hides in a stereotype of the American Dream, the larger context of age and experience redawns to show the way back into history, into complexity.

Most of Albee's plays invert traditional male and female roles. Beyond the immediate satire on the dominating female lies the serious suggestion that the elemental passion abandoned by the rational male may return with the force of demons to convict him of dehumanization. For the antidote is not a complete reversal but an incorporation of the other's values. As Agnes speculates, aspiring to a man's simple world would be futile if the sexes, after all, are reversing. Albee strongly condemns those women who have merely turned sex into power: Nurse who flirts with Intern but refuses, in their suggestive language, to allow his tangent to become a radius to her circumference; the Mommies who have made the Daddies sexless and will-less; and the Long-Winded Lady whose comments on her husband's penis, "trained-back" rather than circumcised, reflects her dread of disorderly or unclean sex.

But Martha and Alice in the model are almost bi-sexual, earth goddesses that comfort, absorb, and renew the flexible heroes George and Julian, even as they reject or devour the unimaginative Nick and the sweatless Lawyer. Imagery of the womb is common in the Gothic experience, as Leslie Fiedler points out, and the Gothic hero is one who is willing to suspend reason, to take the chance that womb will not become tomb, that the castle keep, the hidden room, or the secret garden will be an outlet into a new experience rather than a dead end.

In *The Zoo Story*, male-female inversion is performed by Jerry who communicates with Peter by adopting a feminine role (receiving the knife-phallus is a common experience of the Gothic heroine, just as suicide and seduction were often linked in the sentimental novel) and by acting out the implications of his name (slang for chamber pot) with Peter (slang for penis). The maze of reversed directions in the play is further tribute to the healing power of inversion. Jerry's point throughout is that some conclusions, as well as locations, can be reached only indirectly, the way of passion of the archetypal female, rather than by male reason.

The most sustained thematic inversion in Albee's plays is the Gothic mechanism of the Black Mass in *Who's Afraid of Virginia Woolf?* Satanic ritual is announced by the title of act 2, "Walpurgisnacht," but it exists throughout the play as a parody of the Christian mass. The Black Mass, according to popular tradition, consists of orgies during which there is sexual intercourse with Satan, mock "confession" of evil done, desecration of the Christian sacrament, and parts of the Christian liturgy acted out in distorted ways. Occasionally the tradition mentions human sacrifice and cannibalism, in extreme cases the eating of infants. The events in Albee's play could be described as an orgy, the climax of which comes in the union of Nick and Martha. George twice associates Martha with Satan. When the guests arrive, Martha is "a devil with language," and when she tramples on his past, she is a "satanic bitch." And he cuts her most deeply by calling her a monster, a beast. The association of Martha with Satan rather than the more logical Nick (an echo of "Old Nick") shows again the female to whom power has been transferred from the ineffectual male, and Albee's effort to link the healing possibilities of Black Magic with those of the archetypal earth mother.

Confession is important because it leads to the game George calls "Humiliate the Host," suggesting that part of the Black Mass when the Christian Host is spat upon or misused. But George, the Host, is also the priest who performs the exorcism early that Sunday morning, with Martha in her "chapel dress." Their illusory child is the sacrifice that is central to the ceremony, though not the object of exorcism. For in sacrificing their "Bean bag" they are—as in the Christian Sacrifice—effecting its transformation and assuring its perpetuation. The exorcism itself is the ceremony whereby the contemporary devils Nick and Honey—the clichés of science and its frigid, sterile bride—are cast out. In fact, the entire progress of the final section seems so inevitable, so ceremonial, that one questions whether it is new to George and Martha and ends with that evening. Perhaps the inverted Mass is a regular event, like Martha's raising of her skirts for interesting young faculty men, an event she and George are condemned to perform over and over again with each new set of guests. And perhaps this Satanic ceremony, however playfully it is approached, is their only indication of possibility in a Godless world.

Inversion is carried out in all the plays through language. Clichés are inverted to drop us, as the Gothic trapdoor drops the innocent hero, into a new dimension. *The American Dream* is Albee's most ambitious experiment with language. On one level the twists of language into the unexpected are intended to show our poverty of social discourse, a common theme of the Theater of the Absurd since Ionesco plays like *The Bald Soprano*. But in the very process of inversion, dead language is made alive, and once alive, it magnifies individual possibilities. When Mrs. Barker is told about the "bumble of joy," and step by step the clichéd figures of speech she uses ("Well I hope they cut its tongue out!") become literal, historical events, the effect is as if cliché is made powerful again as language through the agency of Grandma. By her, the incantation of cliché has borne fruit, and the word again becomes the thing. Perhaps even the lie about the van man comes true in the end, transformed from a vague threat to a promising actuality. Ultimately in *The American Dream* the audience and author share a rebirth that is denied to Mommy and Daddy and Mrs. Barker. But Grandma, never taken seriously by the others, is our link with their unawareness. Ironically, she is most alive in her asides, her comments that are wasted on all but the audience.

In *Who's Afraid of Virginia Woolf?* Nick "comes alive" as a threat to George much as the American Dream materializes in the earlier play. But this also is under George's control, for the cliché must be made real before it can be exorcized. At first the rhetoric between History and Biology is only a game, but Nick falls into the trap and threatens: "I'll play the charades like you've got 'em set up . . . I'll play in your language . . . I'll be what you say I am." And then: "I'll show you something come to life you'll wish you hadn't set up." George's childishly clichéd challenge to Nick, "That's for me to know and you to find out," becomes ominously true when Nick discovers the secrets of the imagined child. But George and Martha, unlike Mommy and Daddy, are in full control of their creation, and they gull their guests into feelings of power before they are sent home defeated.

On the stage of *Tiny Alice* cliché is alive in stock Gothic characters, vampire-like, who take from the beginning full control of the human character Julian, as if chessmen had begun to play the player. "Abstractions *are* upsetting," Lawyer says before the fire in the chapel and I take him and Albee literally even though their sympathies are opposite. Abstraction overturns the natural world, subordinating the human to the shadow of the institution that feeds on the human and marries it to its design. Albee attacks institutionalized cliché, just as older Gothic attacked the institutions of clergy and privileged aristocracy, portraying them as the undead that feed on the living. But Albee's play is not an allegory, and we are asked to reject that approach just as Julian finally rejects the rules of the game these shadows try to force on him, the either-or of model-replica, rational-irrational, abstraction-symbol, and God-Alice. Ironically, he accepts his martyrdom on the level of his own psychological need that they have guessed and used against him (the vampire, by popular tradition, must be invited to make its first visit) and transcends it on the theological level, for his faith makes their empty promises real. The reader is asked to believe in the same magic, for the ceremony of Alice is the ceremony of reading the play itself.

In the Gothic novel, reduction and inversion are often preludes to that shock of recognition which causes one character to identify with his double or counterpart. Psychologically this identification indicates a movement toward wholeness, an integration of the psyche. Of course one can refuse to acknowledge the mirror image or be insufficiently developed to recognize it. In older Gothic novels, identification sometimes occurs between innocent hero (or heroine) and villain in a moment when the one realizes that he is not immune from the other's guilt. In William Godwin's *Caleb Williams* (1794), the boy Caleb pursues Falkland's guilt until that man's confession turns the tables and Caleb is infected with guilt and pursued by the older man. Infection of guilt was for eighteenth-century Gothic writers the equivalent of, even as it was a reaction against, the infection of sympathy and benevolence in the novel of sensibility. Both assumed levels of communication beyond the rational, an extra-sensory awareness. The means of identification is often a gradual awareness of similarities through a prolonged confrontation, though the actual recognition may come in a moment of intense emotion or even violence. Often a confession is involved, and sometimes that confession becomes the major vehicle of recognition, as in Coleridge's *The Rime of the Ancient Mariner* and Albee's *The Zoo Story*.

In Albee's play, Peter's complacency is shattered by Jerry's story about the dog. Albee indicates that Jerry's words should "achieve a hypnotic effect on Peter," and further stage directions midway through the monologue reveal that "Peter seems to be hypnotized." At the end, we are told Peter is "disturbed" and "numb." He says, much as the Wedding Guest to the Ancient Mariner, "Why did you tell me all of this?" Jerry, on the other hand, is "suddenly cheerful," Albee says.

During the course of his monologue, Jerry says that it is necessary to establish a relationship with "SOMETHING. With a bed, with a cockroach, with a mirror . . . no, that's too hard, that's one of the last steps." The experience with Peter is that last step for Jerry, spiritually as well as physically. In Gothic fiction the mirror is a horror to the evil one because it either will not reflect him at all, showing his lack of substance, or because it will show him as he really is, something other than human. But Jerry is also Peter's mirror, and Peter's denial of Jerry's story shows a failure to acknowledge publicly that he sees the story is also true for him. Jerry's verbal acknowledgement of the mirror is the final line of the play, an echo of Peter's repeated exclamation, "Oh my God." Albee describes this line as "a combination of scornful mimicry and supplication." Even as he mocks Peter, Jerry has accepted the Peter in himself, and his cry to God is half a prayer that He exists, or that He may be generated through acts of human communication.

Identification in *The Sandbox* and *The American Dream* is a mockery because of the two-dimensional similarity of Mommy and Daddy, but in each play Grandma and the young man, counterparts of age and youth, function to counteract that mockery. In *The Sandbox*, Mommy and Daddy set a pattern of fixity: Daddy's questions, and Mommy's recurring answer, "of course." Their clichés reach absurdity at the moment they suppose Grandma has died: "Brave Mommy," Daddy says. "Brave Daddy," Mommy echoes. They are united only in their shallow responses to a tragic situation. Grandma is something of a stereotype too, but there is life and wit in her caustic comments about Mommy and her flirtation with the young man, a beach boy who has been instructed by someone to play the Angel of Death and does so without in the least comprehending the role. There is life in him to, and Grandma's remark, "you've got a quality," is not wholly sarcastic. The play ends with "his hands on top of Grandma's," Albee directs.

The situation of *The Sandbox* is enlarged in *The American Dream*, but Mommy and Daddy are still two-dimensional, and the young man and Grandma again form the only meaningful alliance in the play as he shares her secret exit. Instances of defensive doubling reinforce the mockery of shallow American materialism. The two hats and the two sons provide for Mommy and Daddy a way out of their frustrations. The second version of each is actually identical to the first, but the need for "satisfaction" demands they be seen as improvements. In the first conversation of the play Mommy and Daddy refer to the "they" who are supposed to arrive, and when Mrs. Barker appears, she refers to herself as "we." Pluralization here, as in *Tiny Alice* and *A Delicate Balance*, shields against individuation. On the other hand, Grandma's wit—especially effective in her moments of introspection—allows her to transcend her clichéd environment, for she sees reality continually on two levels, as illustrated in her puns and in her consciousness of acting a role. Her exit at the end is not a genuine exit but a movement out of the drama to her true position as chorus, seen by the audience and unseen by the characters.

The Death of Bessie Smith satirizes Southern types and the inertia of Southern institutions, but toward the end Nurse is moved emotionally.

Intern has told her earlier in the play of his fantasy in which she stabs herself accidentally in the arm with a letter opener and comes to his emergency station where he holds her and watches "blood coming out of you like water out of a faucet." When Nurse first hears of the accident in which Bessie's arm was almost torn off, she responds for a moment with sympathy and echoes the words applied earlier to her: "like water from a faucet . . . ? Oh, that is terrible." Later she identifies with Bessie's singing: "A dead nigger lady . . . WHO SINGS. Well . . . I sing, too, boy . . . I sing real good." Sarcasm here, as in *The Zoo Story*, does not completely mask the final moments of recognition. Bessie and Nurse have both cracked up, and Nurse knows that her emotional death is as terrible as Bessie's physical death. In admitting this much she has somewhat qualified the irony of her position at the Admissions Desk and transcended the original reduction of her emotions.

The climate of similarity established between the couples in *Who's Afraid of Virginia Woolf?*, particularly the illusory pregnancies of Honey and Martha, sets up the later recognition of their differences. The couples are not true counterparts, like Jerry and Peter, nor reflections like the couples in *A Delicate Balance*. In one sense Nick and Honey are scapegoats summoned to the ceremony as projections of George and Martha's fears of impersonality and barrenness, and cast out accordingly during the exorcism. In another sense the reaction of the guests is as important as Peter's in *The Zoo Story:* the shock of the encounter itself dismisses them as inadequate. In either case, George and Martha use Nick and Honey to reaffirm their marriage by the magic of illusion, not a particular illusory son who is subject to death, but the continual possibilities of illusion itself. There will be other particular illusions and other sacrifices in the cycle of history they have elected over the safer alternative offered by Nick, the leveling of humanism through biological specialization. In act 3 George and Martha cast themselves playfully in roles from Tennessee Williams's *A Streetcar Named Desire*, subscribing to Williams's paradox of the necessity of illusion even as it is necessarily being destroyed by the world's Stanleys or Nicks.

The model in *Tiny Alice* represents the dimensions of possibility and reflects the quality of action in the play. It comes to life three times during the play, during the fire, during the "ceremony of Alice," and during Julian's death agony. In each case it is called into activity by events in the drama: the argument between Miss Alice and Lawyer over her passion, the wedding of Julian to Alice, and Julian's acceptance of priesthood. Only in the last case—Julian's decision—is sound created and the thing fully and sensually alive. What the others see as a trap Julian sees as a Christian paradox of life in death. He alone faces the full implications of the double dimension. They can act out each other's roles—hence the plays within the play—but their identification with each other is always clichéd and defensive, and they are limited by their refusal to believe in the paradox they insist upon for Julian. They are trapped by their particular professions, but he escapes from his original professional limitation as a lay brother, celibacy without priesthood, to the fullness of life implied in a priesthood without celibacy, a condition denied by the Church but possible in the liberated churchman. More clearly than the other plays, *Tiny Alice* illustrates the double thrust of the Gothic, the demysticizing of institutions and the mysticizing of the individual.

In *A Delicate Balance* Agnes and Tobias are mirrored by Edna and Harry who, Albee tells us in listing the players, they are "very much like." Edna and Harry's crisis of despondency and fear corresponds to a similar crisis in Agnes and Tobias's past. Having lost one son they became afraid of having another, and therefore of life itself. Tobias "spilled" his seed on Agnes's belly, and their defenses mustered to insure immunity from further emotion. But the inversions brought by the uninvited guests have spilled things again, shattering immunity. Agnes is proud of her "double vision" that allows her to be both in and out of a situation, but this double view is actually a protection against what Edna calls "the double demand of friendship." Edna, more advanced in fear and less defensive than Agnes, sums up the horror of recognition: "It's sad to come to the end of it, isn't it, nearly the end; so much more of it gone by . . . than left, and still not know—still not have learned . . . the boundaries, what we may not do . . . not ask, for fear of looking in a mirror." With the leaving of Edna and Tobias, and the morning that has restored reason and safety again, Agnes's control returns, and her final speech is somewhat like her opening sentence. But now she has slipped from saying she *might* one day lose her mind to saying she *will* lose her mind. And instead of being astonished about Claire's ingratitude, the point of her opening speech, she is now astonished about the daylight, the reason and order of things. She talks from wonder, rather than from cliché. Their cycle of control and lack of control will continue, but their confrontation with their doubles has left Agnes and Tobias closer to each other, and to the fears and possibilities of their buried life.

The only character to change in *Box* and *Quotations from Chairman Mao Tse-Tung* is Long-Winded Lady. In talking out her past to the silent minister, she reveals her coldness and fear, and the subtle clichés of her buried life are played against the blatant clichés of Mao and Old Woman. Whether she is conscious of this counterpoint is not immediately clear, but her attitude changes from wonder at her fall itself to a questioning of her motives. She reviews the scene after the fall when passengers asked if she had fallen on purpose, and she ends with her answer which, in the light of her "confession" to the minister takes on new meaning: "Good heavens, no; *I* have nothing to die for." Beneath the outraged optimism appears the crack in her box, the futility of death that argues the futility of life.

Reduction, inversion, and recognition are not exclusive to Gothic works. They are common movements in drama or fiction whereby a controlled experience tests and rewards someone with awareness, as in the initiation story. Or in non-fiction like *Walden* that stresses emotional development. But Albee's imaginative use of these categories to bring out the resonances of cliché, his fascination with mystery, the mating of counterparts, and the summoning of unknown powers and shadows, his popular contempt for reason and intellect, his exaggerated attack on the abstracted institutions that prey on humans, and finally, his refusal to dismiss as mere absurdities the bizarre and grotesque—all these indicate his affinity with Gothic writing. Gothic has never been a school so much as an attitude, not so much a form as a technique for depicting, as Albee does, the horrors and the possibilities we fashion for ourselves from the homeliest, as well as the strangest material.

RONALD HAYMAN

All Over

All Over, written between August and November 1970, is Albee's first full-length play for over four years. It has roots in *A Delicate Balance* and in *Boz* and *Quotations from Chairman Mao Tse-Tung*, while it also bears a certain resemblance to Ionesco's *Le Roi se meurt*, though the dying man who is central to Albee's play never has a word to speak, only a death rattle just before the final curtain. The play is partly about the effects that the death is having on the people whose lives have been most dependent on his—wife, mistress, children and best friend—and it is partly about death and dying in general. The effective absence of the central character helps to generalize the subject matter. So do the seniority and the anonymity of all seven speakers. The Wife is seventy-one, the Mistress sixty-one, the Son fifty-two, the Daughter forty-five, the Best Friend seventy-three, the Doctor eighty-six and the Nurse sixty-five. None of them will have much to do in the future except rake over the embers of the past. The Son and Daughter have as little to look forward to as the others. They are both flabby, undynamic: the vitality seems to have been drained out of them by their parents.

The play is more a conversation than an action. Albee is not primarily concerned with developing the relationships between his characters. The Wife's rapprochement with the Mistress and her estrangement from her Son and Daughter have begun long before the action starts and if they go further, this is only incidental. The various clashes between the characters contribute substantially to the tensions which keep the audience's interest alive but in

From *Contemporary Playwrights: Edward Albee*. © 1971 by Ronald Hayman. A.D. Peters & Co. Ltd. and Heinemann Educational Books, 1971.

67

so far as the dialogue explores the characters, the exploration is almost entirely verbal and retrospective. In fact the play is mainly a threnody, not on the death of the man in the bed but on the lives of the others who will survive him.

Reading through the script, the conversation falls very clearly into sections and the linkage between them depends on subject matter, not action. In fact, as in *Box* and *Quotations*, the structure is almost musical. The seven voices are like seven instruments which develop each other's themes as one solo section leads into the next. Their music is a carefully cadenced rhetoric, not unlike that of the Long-Winded Lady in *Quotations*, but there is little attempt at a distancing irony here and *All Over* is unlike *Quotations* in making no attempt at differentiating between the speech patterns of the various characters. But at least it is an advantage that the rhythms in the prose are no longer eclectic as they were in *A Delicate Balance*. And certainly the rhetoric provides an effective means of bringing past action vividly to life. The provocatively leisurely, consciously literary sentences, with their clearly notated pauses, their prolonged parentheses and rubato stresses create subtle tensions in the confrontations between the characters and subtle relationships between past and present.

> THE WIFE: When I came there, to the hospital—the last time,
> before the . . . removal here—I said . . .
> (*Turns to* THE MISTRESS.)
> you were not there, were shopping, or resting, I think . . .
> (*Turns back generally.*)
> looking at him, all wired up, I stood at the foot of the
> bed—small talk all gone, years ago—I shook my head,
> and I clucked I'm afraid—tsk-tsk-tsk-tsk—for he opened
> his eyes a little, baleful, as I suppose my gaze must have
> seemed to him, though it was merely . . . objective. This
> won't do at all, I said. Wouldn't you rather be somewhere
> else? Do you want to be here? He kept his eyes half open
> for a moment or so, then closed them, and nodded his
> head, very slowly. Well, which? I said, for I realized I'd
> asked two questions, and a nod could mean either yes or
> no. Which is it?, I said; do you want to be here? Slow
> shake of the head. You *would* rather be somewhere else.
> Eyes opened and closed, twice, in what I know—from
> eons—to be impatience; then . . . nodding. Well,
> naturally, I said, in my bright business tone, of course

you don't want to be here. Do you want to go home? No
reply at all, the eyes burning at me. Your own home, I
mean, not mine certainly. Or hers, Perhaps you want to
go there. Shall I arrange something? Eyes still on me, no
movement. Do you want *her* to arrange it? Still the eyes,
still no movement. Has it been arranged? Has she
arranged it already? The eyes lightened; I could swear
there was a smile in them. She *has*. Well; good. I have—
mind you—I have . . . there is no intent in me . . . if it is
done, splendid. All I care is whether it is *done*. I no longer
feel possessive, have not for . . . and the eyes went out—
stayed open, went out, as they had . . . oh . . . so often;
so far back.

Even when there is violent action in the past, as in the Best Friend's
speech about his mad wife, the emotion is distanced.

It was after I decided not to get the divorce, that year,
until . . . before I, before I committed her. Each thing,
each . . . incident—uprooting all the roses, her hands so
torn, so . . . killing the doves and finches . . . setting fire
to her hair . . . all . . . all those times, those things I
knew were pathetic and not wanton, I watched myself
withdraw, step back and close down some portion of . . .
THE MISTRESS: Ah, but that's not the same.

The Best Friend has been saying that he had been observing the same kind
of withdrawal in himself that the Wife had so often noticed in her husband's
eyes: this is characteristic of the way Albee grafts one section of his conversation on to the next.

Occasionally there are outcrops of violent action in the present, as when
the Wife and the Daughter exchange slaps, or when, at the end of act 1, the
Wife and the Mistress converge like ferocious animals on the photographers
and reporters whom the Daugher has vengefully admitted into the room.
But the violent moments seem almost irrelevant to the conversation and
because it is not integrated, the emphasis on the animality of the women at
the end of act 1 seems overstressed and reminiscent of what Pinter was doing
in *The Homecoming*.

What seems to have its roots in *Quotations* (or in the experience that led
to it) is the preoccupation with death and dying, the insistence on the difference between the two and the concern with the question of the age at

which one becomes aware of death. (In *Quotations* it is thirty-nine; in *All Over* thirty-eight.) The action of *All Over* is the inaction of waiting for death, but unlike the inaction of *Waiting for Godot* it does not make a point of focusing on the fact of passivity. The play might be better if it did. The process of the old man's dying produces a suspension in seven other lives (incuding those of the Doctor and the Nurse, who are also sporadically seen to be doing their jobs) but the suspension is not the real subject of the play, only the pretext for prolonging the conversation. In *Quotations* no pretext was needed: the play established a convention which told us to expect nothing but talk and the contrasts between the three styles of monologue satisfied our appetite for variety. This method could probably not be made to work in a full-length play, and though it is good to see Albee trying to introduce some of the stylization typical of his off-Broadway work into a play written for Broadway, it is impossible to be satisfied with this particular compromise. There is one line, the Wife's phrase "The little girl I was when he came to me," which is used as a refrain, very much in the manner of *Quotations*, but even this degree of abstraction (superimposed on the naturalistic surface by making the Wife seem abstracted when she repeats the line) quarrels with the attempts—perfunctory though they are—at creating theatrical suspense of the conventional kind. The only conflict which has to be resolved by a decision is provided by the arguments between the Wife, the Mistress, and the Best Friend about whether the corpse should be buried or cremated. These are very skilfully developed but it not this sort of skill that the play needs. Albee has proved again and again his gift for electrifying his dialogue with high tension antagonism. But the main failure of *All Over* is the failure to mould the conversation into a satisfying shape. The culmination of the play's action is the death we have all been waiting for since the curtain went up on act 1, while the conversation, which ought to have been able to compensate for this by working up to a good climax, merely peters out. The Wife and the Mistress have been asking each other how they will face the future, but in answering they have reminisced about the past in very much the same way as they have all through the play.

The two women's liking for each other and the antagonism they both feel towards the Son and the Daughter could have been exploited much more fully, but—partly because the Wife and the Mistress are so similar to each other in the way they talk and apparently think—they are never differentiated sufficiently for the relationship between them to become more than super-ficially compelling. Albee tells us that the Wife is a typical wife who has never loved more than one man, and that the Mistress is a typical mistress who since childhood has never fallen in love with a man who hasn't belonged to another woman. They discuss the question of whether the roles they have played in this man's life could have been reversed if the Mistress had met him before the Wife and they agree that they couldn't. The rhetoric serves admirably to sharpen the surface tension between the two women and the conclusion of their argument convinces us but it has too little substantiation in action to involve us.

If the attitudes of these two are rather over-explained, the Wife's attitude to her children is rather under-explained. The disgust she feels for them arouses our curiosity. In the scene between the two of them at the beginning of act 2, Albee shows more of them from their own point of view and we see that they both disgust themselves. They are failures in their own eyes, desperately in need of love and off-puttingly aware of their own unlovableness. The Daughter is very much a continuation of the Daughter in *A Delicate Balance*. Aggressive in proportion to her vulnerability, she makes the same kind of clumsy, self-pitying demonstrations, as if to advertise her immaturity. The Son is seriously under-written. It is curious that after Albee had derided so many married couples for failing to produce a male child, the first son to appear in his plays should be a disappointing fifty-two-year-old whose disappointingness is taken so much for granted.

The Doctor and the Nurse are still less satisfactory because still less integral to what the play is really about. The Doctor is given a nice line in keeping an eye on his patient while nearly nodding off to sleep; the Nurse is the means of providing one of the play's most theatrical moments, when the dying man hemorrhages and she comes into view with her white uniform spotted with blood. But it is a mistake to try to fit her into the main pattern with a gratuitous announcement that she was once the mistress of the Doctor's dead son, a doctor who had imposed his own timing on death by killing himself when he realized that he was suffering from an incurable cancer. Like so many of the other set speeches of the Doctor and the Nurse, this piece of narrative is too obviously just another variation on the main theme. So is the Doctor's long speech—effective enough in itself—about prisoners in death cells masturbating to a fantasy of the executioner. And so is the Nurse's comment about the way the public could "share in" Pope John's death as it could not share in the more sudden deaths of Jack and Robert Kennedy.

There is almost nothing in the play which is not effective—locally. The Best Friend's narrative about an encounter with his mad wife in a car is a virtuoso piece of writing.

"Hello," I said, "how are you?," realizing as I said it that if she laughed in my face, or screamed, or went for me I would not have been surprised. She smiled, though, and stroked the fur beside her cheek with the back of her hand. Her voice was calm, and extremely . . . rested. "It's fine in here," she said, "how is it out there?" I didn't reply: I was so aware of her eyes on me, and her sister's, and the attendant not turned, but looking straight ahead, and smoking. She went on: "Oh, it would be so nice to say to you "come closer, so I can whisper something to you." That way I could put my hand to the back of your head and say very softly, 'Help me'; either that or rub my lips against your ear, the way you like, and then *grab* you with my teeth, and hold on as you pulled away, blood, and ripping." It was so . . . objective, and without rancour, I didn't move at all; the attendant did, I remember; she turned. "I can't do that, though," my wife said—sadly, I think. "Do you know why?" "No, I don't know why." "Because," she said, "when I look at your ear I see the rump and the tail of a mouse coming out from it; he must be chewing very deeply." I didn't move; my fingers stayed where they were. It could be I was trying to fashion some reply, but there *is* none to that. Her sister gunned the motor then; having seen me when she parked, she must have thought to keep it idling. "Nice to see you," she said to me, the same grim smile, mad eyes, and she backed out, curving, shifted, and moved off. And what I retain of their leaving, most of all, above the mouse, my wife, *myself*, for that matter, is the sound of her sister's bracelet clanking against the steering wheel—a massive gold chain with a disc suspended from it, a large thin disc, with her first name, in facsimile, scrawled across one face of it; that; clanking as she shifted.

But not only is it irrelevant: it creates an atmosphere which has little in common with the atmosphere that ought to be prevailing in the room. In fact it helps to diffuse it. The effect it makes is a very considerable one, but it is just one of a series of very considerable effects which do not quite constitute a play.

Nevertheless, *All Over* provides reason for being rather more sanguine about Albee's future than we have had the right to be for some years. His only two previous attempts at a fusion between his off-Broadway experimentalism and his Broadway naturalism were *Tiny Alice* and *A Delicate Bal-*

ance: the new play is a more honest piece of writing than the former and more original than the latter. He is still one of the most powerful influences in the American theatre, although he has not yet equalled the success of *Who's Afraid of Virginia Woolf?* and his three adaptations seriously damaged his reputation. The rival pulls of Beckett and Broadway have brought his talent dangerously near to disintegrating but there is still hope that it will recover.

ANTHONY HOPKINS

Conventional Albee: Box *and* Chairman Mao

There is little in Edward Albee's play(s) *Box* and *Quotations from Chairman Mao Tse-Tung* that obviously conforms to even an expressionistically liberal definition of "normal" drama. Such things as plot, character, setting, dramatic conflict, dialogue hardly exist in any conventional sense. In *Box* there is only the stark outline of a large cube and the epithets from a disembodied female voice. The set directions for *Chairman Mao* specify *"the deck of an ocean liner,"* but the outline cube from *Box* also remains present throughout. Of the four characters in *Chairman Mao*, one—the Minister—never speaks, and the others utter interleaved but essentially independent monologues. Part way through the play the Voice from *Box* begins to be heard as well and, like a reprise, lines from *Box* end the play(s).

Nevertheless, it remains that there is a good deal here that is characteristic of Albee's practices in the body of his work generally. Symbols, images, ideas, characters, and not infrequently formal techniques, mark *Box* and *Chairman Mao* as continuations and extensions of, rather than radical departures from Albee's usual complex of interests.

Boxes, for example, are frequently prominent in Albee plays. In *The Zoo Story*, Jerry keeps "a small strongbox without a lock which has in it . . . sea-rounded rocks I picked up on the beach when I was a kid" and some letters, pathetic, ragged remnants of his miserable existence. Grandma in *The American Dream* is busy boxing up, to take with her, everything of value in the apartment. Her boxes contain

From *Modern Drama* 16, no. 2 (September 1973). © 1973 by the University of Toronto, Graduate Centre for Study of Drama.

> some old letters, a couple of regrets . . . Pekinese . . . blind at
> that . . . the television . . . my Sunday teeth . . . eighty-six years
> of living . . . some sounds . . . a few images, a little garbled by
> now . . . and, well . . . [*she shrugs*] . . . you know . . . the things
> one accumulates.

In both cases the boxes seem to suggest arbitrary coherence for experience perhaps otherwise random and chaotic.

The Sandbox contains Albee's first sustained exploitation of the symbolic potentiality of the box image. Richly evocative, it is both womb and coffin, suggestive of the earth from which all men come and to which all return, and of the enforced sterility and imposed senility afflicting Grandma. Its arbitrary, artificial structure in one way contrasts with the free open expanse of the beach, yet is is also the fortress in which Grandma seeks to defend her integrity against the onslaughts of her daughter.

In addition, many of Albee's locations and settings implicitly or deliberately stress a box-like claustrophobia. This tendency perhaps reaches its apotheosis in the rooms within rooms and models within models within *Tiny Alice*. But the many small rooms of Jerry's rooming house are like so many boxes, as are the animal cages he sees as representative of all the artificial separations in the world. Four times, Albee chooses as his setting the box-like dimensions of the conventional living room. Projected publicly by their inhabitants as enclosures of order, stability, harmony, the living rooms of *The American Dream*, *Virginia Woolf*, *A Delicate Balance*, and *Everything in the Garden* all prove to be pressurized containers of explosive hatred, duplicity, self-deceit, and fear.

The skeletal cube of *Box*, therefore, may be seen as a consciously abstract example of one of Albee's favored images of the nature of contemporary life. In *Box*, the cube is environment—personal, familial, social, somatic, psychic, private, public, local, national—from the least to the most inclusive levels simultaneously. It is the life space of each man and of all mankind. The cube is the park bench, the living rooms, Alice's castle, the sandbox, Jerry's and Grandma's boxes all refined away to essential outline.

The Voice is the articulated expression of the quality of life within the life space. The images it uses, the stories, or parts of stories it tells, are the metaphoric utterances of a sense of decay, decline, destruction; of the end of honesty, vitality, morality, hope, and purpose. The Voice is George's reading from *The Decline of the West*, Grandma's inarticulate but meaningful cries, Julian's anguished cries of isolation and abandonment now purged of passion and expectation. The Voice is the emotion of total collapse; it talks of unreal hopes in the past, the total devastation of all values in the present, and is unable even to contemplate the future.

Inherently, the box seems capable of providing the opportunity for a life well-ordered, satisfying, meaningful: "Room to rock. And room to move about . . . some, Enough." It has, however, suffered spiritual debasement. Craft has replaced art, the lesser, less worthy activity has supplanted the greater. No longer are there goals and ideals, only activity for its own sake, process without direction or purpose. This opposition, created at the beginning of the play is essentially that which is developed throughout the remainder of *Box*, except that more stress becomes placed upon images of death and waste, especially with respect to nature and to art.

The seven hundred million babies need not be, for example, literally dead. The image is one of generally misdirected and therefore useless energy, and could equally as well represent the waste of masturbation or Tobias's seed useless upon Agnes's belly. The spilled milk also impresses as an exemplification of deficient virtue and the corrupt misapplication of creative and generative energies. It may take its origin from the situation wherein farmers pour their milk on the ground because payment for it will not be satisfactorily high while, at the same time, children in Asia and America suffer malnutrition, but its significance is not restricted to such a situation only. It relates directly to the Papal Injunction against the sin of affluence while most of the world is in need; and to the destructive effect of any refusal to give that which should be given. Also, the idea of spilled milk is used to develop the concept of the inadequacy of substitution. Cash donations will not effectively replace a lack of human commitment, a profusion of gifts and material goods cannot compensate for a dearth of emotional engagement, CARE packages do not satisfy the need for human love.

Central to the experience of major characters in several of Albee's plays is the collapse of that which is most precious to life and most necessary for survival. In most cases, it is a framework of illusion that crumbles under the pressure of reality. Peter loses forever his comfortable isolation from raw experience, the Nurse in *Bessie Smith* is traumatically stripped of her illusions of attractiveness and white respectability, George and Martha lose the delusions they use to account for and excuse their failure; Julian finally must question his unquestionable assumption that God exists.

In this play, the most powerful expression of the collapse of life centres on the collapse of the compensatory function of art. The basis of this notion is that the aesthetic quality of art, its internal order and harmony, its creative beauty is (or should be) a form of spiritual refreshment, an uplifting experience that compensates for the inevitable disharmony and failure of raw life, an inspiration that, unlike illusions, which permit a retreat from life, helps to restore hope and confidence and the courage to grapple with the problems of life and existence.

As the Voice expresses it, art no longer is able to maintain this function. The beauty of art is now such a total contrast to, so totally unlike and unrelated to the world in which it exists, that it serves now only to reinforce, intensify, and increase the sense of fruitlessness, waste, and decay:

> When art begins to hurt . . . it's time to look around.

> When the beauty of it reminds us of *loss*, instead of the attainable.

> When art hurts.

> Then the corruption is complete.

And when art hurts, the beauty of nature can be only a nostalgic memory. Flocks of birds and monarch butterflies, aesthetic, dynamic order in nature, nature's art, also lose their inspirational and restorative function. They remind only of what once was, what is now unattainable. Both civilization and nature, in an atmosphere of emptiness analagous to the aftermath of a nuclear holocaust, suffer from total spiritual devastation and are rendered useless, powerless, devoid of meaning. All that remains is *"the sound of bell buoys and sea gulls,"* the harsh cries of chaos, storm and fear.

In discussing *Quotations from Chairman Mao Tse-Tung* it is convenient, given the nature of its monologue interweaving, to discuss each speaker in turn.

Equally, it is convenient to begin with the monologue spoken by the Old Woman, for the poem she recites has more obvious coherence and development in conventional terms than the speeches of the other characters. The poem "Over the Hill to the Poor House" deals with one of Albee's most persistent dramatic topics, the rejection of the old by the young, used here, as elsewhere, to suggest ruthless inhumanity and selfishness, emotional and spiritual decay, the consequent futility of the future, and the demise of all worthy impulses, effort and values.

The poem contains a sentimentalized version of a biography similar to that of previous grandmother characters. Strong, vigorous, independent, attractive in her youth, the lady in the poem, when she is old, is progressively rejected by her children. Her years of love, devotion and sacrifice reap only loneliness, suffering, and total betrayal. And although we learn nothing directly of the old woman character who recites the poem, her general appearance and demeanor—"Shabby, poor . . . She has a bag [box?] with her. An orange; an apple, one or two cans"—is appropriate to the character in the poem and the other grandmother characters.

The Long-Winded Lady is perhaps Albee's most dismally devastating picture of a "mature" woman. She is Martha and Agnes without the protection of their hard emotional shells, she is self-centred Mommy turned neurotic and in retreat from life. She has three major complementary and intertwined stories to tell; of the death of her husband, the decadence of her daughter, and her own experience of falling from a ship.

The ship she fell from, and the one she is presently on, are settings reminiscent of Albee's early plays. In *The Zoo Story, The Death of Bessie Smith* and *The Sandbox*, the action takes place in front of a background that is deliberately open and bare. Peter's park bench is set against open sky, not buildings, the sky is explicitly meant to suggest openness and space in *Bessie Smith*, and Grandma's enclosed life is set against the open expanse of sea and sand and sky. The ocean liner deck similarly expresses a sense of life as a small structured particle in a formless universe. Beyond the railing of the ship, open sea and sky merge at the horizon of infinity and eternity, as the ship, without obvious destination, simply travels aimlessly on.

The Long-Winded Lady relates her tales with bemused surprise that increasingly reveals a lack of empathy and intelligence. When she saw a taxi run amuck, the still hot crullers remained more important to her than the deaths of ten or twelve people, which she saw, but did not really react to. Repeatedly in her rambling narratives she attempts, and pathetically fails to philosophize on the meaining of what has happened to her. At one point she will say of herself: "One is suddenly leaning on one's imagination—which is poor support, let me tell you . . . at least in *my* case—learning on that, which doesn't last for long, and over one goes!"

Talking of her fall, she is led to remember her husband, a man "neat; accurate; precise. In everything. All our marriage. Except dying. Except that . . . dreadful death." Apart from his final significant participation in life, he otherwise embodied the qualities she prized in life: quiet, calm, ease, a sense of control, the complete absence of anything large, random, erratic, challenging. In her preference for civilized ease, the Lady reminds one of Peter before he meets Jerry, and with her preference for withdrawal, of Julian.

But her husband did insist on dying, and unlike the deaths caused by the taxi, his progressive inner corruption from cancer could neither be avoided nor dismissed. Neither death nor dying had previously been allowed to be part of the Lady's idea of life, partly because as truly significant aspects of life they demanded active participation, adjustment to reality, courage, fortitude and inner strength. Unwilling, unable, to incorporate death, and especially the process of dying, into her miniscule universe, the Lady is left now only a selfish sense that her husband almost purposely abandoned her to drift in a world she does not wish to confront and is essentially unequipped to cope with.

Frequently with Albee, the failure of the present generation is confirmed and consolidated by the next. The inheritors of George and Martha's sterility are Nick and Honey. Julia does her part to totally destroy the institution of the family through repeated marriages and divorces. The American Dream and the Angel of Death naturally and openly possess the psychotic indifference Mommy and Daddy hypocritically cultivate. In *Chairman Mao*, this place is filled by the Long-Winded Lady's forty-odd year old daughter, a Julia gone to complete ruin, living in Mexico with two twenty-year-old houseboys.

Considering the barren futility of her life, and the inadequacy of her resources for dealing with it, the Lady's falling from the ship is, as likely as not, an unconscious suicide attempt. As she has no life, in terms of vitality, and is afraid of the possibility of vitality, she may as well end her frustration and fear by becoming literally dead. Questioned on this point after her rescue, however, she replies with a devastating, innocent parody of the cry of suicidal despair: "Throw myself off? . . . Good heavens, no; I have nothing to die for." If, as is the case with Agnes and Martha and Mommy, this middle-aged female has at least latent symbolic significance as a representative of the spiritual state of adult America, Albee's vision of American moral depravity seems to have considerably worsened. The Long-Winded Lady possesses almost no trace of even perverse energy, is possessed by merely neuraesthenic inertia.

The two female monologists are in many respects, essentially familiar Albee characters in reasonably recognizable Albee situations. The third speaking part in *Chairman Mao*, however, introduces an apparently new persona into the Albee repertoire of characterizations—Mao Tse-Tung, Chairman of the People's Republic of China.

Albee does not give Chairman Mao a personality as such. His speeches are, entirely, direct quotations from the "little red book" of the cultural revolution, *Quotations from Chairman Mao Tse-Tung*, a collection of short selections from the extensive writings of the Chairman. Albee selects from the book with deliberate care, choosing passages immediately impressive as contrastive to the moods of the other monologues. The Chairman's first speech, for example, is taken from chapter twenty-one of the *Quotations* entitled "Self-Reliance and Arduous Struggle." The passage tells a fairy tale of the type of faith which moves mountains. A determined old man and his two sons so persevered in attempting to clear away two large mountains that God sent two angels to remove the mountains. It draws a moral for the Chinese people who must move the two mountains of imperialism and feudalism which oppress them. The story explicitly presents, and endorses, many of the virtues, such as discipline, perseverence, faith, co-operation, courage, that Albee has supported, in varying degrees, throughout his work. They are also, of course, virtues significantly lacking in most Albee characters and situations. In general, the remainder of the *Quotations* used in the play have this same quality—in tones of absolute, confident assertion they express vigor, commitment, purpose, vitality and other heroic virtues that Albee has found either conspicuously absent from the world of which he usually writes or possessed only by the old and dying. Typical of the chosen passages are the following:

> We must give active support to the national independence and liberation movement in Asia, Africa, and Latin America as well as to the peace movement and to the just struggles in all the countries of the world.
>
> A revolution is not a dinner party, or writing an essay, or painting a picture, or doing embroidery; it cannot be so refined, so leisurely and gentle, so temperate, kind, courteous, restrained and magnanimous. A revolution is an insurrection, an act of violence by which one class overthrows another.
>
> People of the world unite and defeat the U.S. aggressors and all their running dogs.

It seems unlikely that such passages, or their speaker, appear in the play for ideological reasons. Albee's usual rage against America is a lover's rage against the beloved's failure to live up to his best self, not an enemy's basic disgust with his opponent. In any case, with no evidence other than the present use of the *Quotations* it would be irresponsible to suggest that Edward Albee has suddenly begun promoting the people's revolution and calling for the overthrow of America.

It seems more plausible to suggest that the anti-U.S. bias contained, at least implicitly in all, and explicitly in many of Mao's speeches is being used by Albee to impress upon his audience the necessity for moral reform within themselves. Mao exists for Albee not as a mouthpiece for political revolution in the U.S., nor as a shock tactic for alerting America to the continued reality of the "red menace," but as a means of forcing viewers to admit the reality of their personal complicity in the decline of values and morals in America. Confronted with the presence of Mao, with his absolute difference from them in all things, they must also become aware of his difference from themselves in terms of inner strength and passion for a cause. The aged Mao is the leader, not the outcast; and he suffers not at all any doubts about the value and purpose of life.

Moreover, Mao, even as character in a play, is inescapably real. (Albee even directs that "*an attempt should be made to make the actor resemble Mao as much as possible.*") George and Martha, Julian and Alice are, after all, only imaginative creations of the artist, Albee's rage only personal insight rather than objective verifiable truth, and an audience, to avoid confronting its own failings, can dismiss even the most morally powerful plays as entertaining fictions.

Such a possibility does not exist with respect to Mao. There is, in reality, a Chairman Mao Tse-Tung of the People's Republic of China. The little red book, and the writings from which it is excerpted really exist, and the moral commitment of Maoist revolutionaries, in China and elsewhere, has been proven in life, repeatedly. Albee has always exhorted his audiences to face reality. By using Mao as a character he denies them the opportunity to avoid that exhortation. Mao is, in the broadest sense, an external counterpart to the social criticism of America Albee has been engaged in, from inside that society, throughout his artistic career.

These two plays, accordingly, although they may perhaps be formal departures from some conventions of dramatic presentation, contain within their boundaries what is essentially an extension of Albee's continuing examination of American moral collapse and ethical decay. In these terms, their most significant feature may be the total absence of hope or redemption they project.

MARY CASTIGLIE ANDERSON

Staging the Unconscious:
Edward Albee's Tiny Alice

Near the end of his lengthy monologue about himself and the dog, Jerry, in Edward Albee's *The Zoo Story*, unleashes a desperate rambling which springs from his deep need to establish contact with something: "If not with people . . . if not with people . . . SOMETHING. With a bed, with a cockroach, with a mirror. . . ." But here he stops: "no, that's too hard, that's one of the last steps." It is approaching this last step that we find the lay brother, Julian, in *Tiny Alice*, Albee's most cryptic play. Julian's odyssey within Miss Alice's house takes him, in fact, *through* the looking glass on a quest for self-discovery, a quest resounding with psychic implication and leading (if we accept the conclusion as epiphany) to a revelation of mythic proportion.

Most critics willing to go beyond Robert Brustein's and George Wellwarth's dismissal of the play as "meaningless" have interpreted its theme as ironic; among them, Anne Paolucci and Ruby Cohn agree on a definition of Alice as "an incomprehensible Nothing" while Lee Baxandall and Leighton M. Ballew see her as simply the manifestation of Julian's need to believe in something, the final irony being that he accepts the man-made symbol of God he so strongly resisted. Harold Clurman pans the play as an ultimately uninteresting effort "to prove the world an intolerably damned place," and only John Gassner is willing to concede that its concern with "the enigmas of life" or "the futility of trying to explain existence rationally" has claimed playwrights' attention from the beginning of literate theatre. Albee himself has said of the ending of *Tiny Alice:*

From *Renascence: Essays on Value in Literature* 33 (1979). © 1979 by the Catholic Renascence Society.

> [Julian] is left with pure abstraction—whatever it be called: God or Alice—and in the end, according to your faith, one of two things happens. Either the abstraction personifies itself, is proven real, or the dying man, in the last necessary effort of self-delusion, creates and believes in what he knows does not exist.

The ironic interpretation remains ultimately unsatisfying, however, especially since in all his drama, most critical interpretations notwithstanding, Albee has never shown himself to be either absurdist or nihilist. In *The Zoo Story*, he portrays the wasteland of modern society in which the chasm between one human being and another has become so vast that Jerry must sacrifice his life in order to bridge it. But, by so doing, he does, in fact, manage to break through Peter's carefully designed cage of false security and self-preservation. The essence of Jerry's communication with Peter at the moment their lives touch is disturbingly transient and enigmatic. Albee questions the substance of one human being's contact with another, but he never doubts that somehow that contact is possible, and he posits unquestioningly that it is essential.

Who's Afraid of Virginia Woolf? is a purgation rite in which George and Martha strip each other of their defenses, illusions, and fictions. The destruction of their metaphorical son provides at least the potential for their rebirth into a new and more authentic relationship where before none had existed. But again, Albee will not define for us the nature of authenticity nor even suggest whether that authenticity can ever be actualized and sustained between George and Martha. His message is only that in order to *begin* we must face our past, admit our illusions and our vulnerability, and accept our fear.

In *Seascape* we find Charlie, who must learn to relinquish the womblike security to which he has retreated (as a child he would descend to a cove at the bottom of the sea where mentally he has remained through is adult life) in order to accept the challenge of assisting a new species, themselves emerging from the sea, to "Begin." In this context, then, it is plausible to give *Tiny Alice*, despite its dark and foreboding tone, and apocalyptic reading.

It has been suggested often enough that the play operates on numerous levels, the simplest being an apparent betrayal story of a man offered by his church to a group of demonic characters for the sum of a hundred million dollars a year for twenty years. The man is sent as an emissary to the house of the donor, an eccentric woman named simply Miss Alice, to "clear up odds and ends." While there, this man, a celibate and ascetic, is lured into a strange and mysterious world by the temptations of wealth, luxury, friendship, and finally sexuality. He is offered happiness in the form of marriage to Miss Alice; but once he accepts he is abandoned by her and her cohorts (including his Cardinal who sent him on the bizarre mission), fatally shot, and left to die alone on the altar of Alice, the mysterious goddess whom they all seem to serve, thus becoming their sacrifice to her.

But the play seen on this level leaves many ambiguities, the chief of which is, perhaps, the role of the three tempters: Lawyer, Butler, and Miss Alice. They seem at first sinister agents of an evil force sent to undermine the virtues of Julian. But often they indicate to him that they are helping him, that the process he is undergoing, painful though it is, is for his own benefit. In the last act, for instance, when Julian asks Butler, "Are you my friend?" Butler responds, "I *am*; yes; but you'll probably think not." In the same scene, Julian insists that all his life he has "fought against the symbol" and Miss Alice tells him, "Then you should be happy now," indicating his struggle is over. We must question, too, whether Julian's virtues, sincere though they seem as far as he is aware of them, are in fact genuine. As he begins to reveal himself to Miss Alice, it becomes apparent that his conscious spirituality has been based all along on a subconscious carnality.

This insistent split demands a more subtle interpretation of the play, one focused on Julian's psychology. The disclosure of Julian's personal unconscious with its powerful, repressed sex drive is prepared for early in *Tiny Alice* by the motif of revealing information (as one would reveal repressed motivations). The first scene between Lawyer and Cardinal is filled with persistent references to secret pasts, dossiers, and the manifestation of defamatory information. When, in the following scene, Julian refuses to reveal to Lawyer the details of his years in the asylum, Lawyer hisses prophetically, "You will . . . in time. Won't he, Butler? Time? The great revealer?"

The action of the drama will unveil the layers of Julian's psyche, from the exposure of his repressed sexuality to the disclosure of the Oedipal drive and the father-son conflict. And beyond that we will find yet a deeper layer— so that we might concur with Miss Alice when she exclaims "expansively" at one point, "Oh, my Julian! How many layers! Yes?" That the play undertakes a journey through his mind is made clear from the very first scene in which Julian appears and describes his experiences in the mental home to Butler: "I . . . declined. I . . . shriveled into myself; a glass dome . . . descended, and it seemed I was out of reach, unreachable, finally unreaching, in this . . . paralysis, of sorts." The model house, the home of Alice, a shriveled version of the real house sealed by a glass dome also appears on stage for the first time in this scene. Clearly, it presents itself to us as a symbol of Julian's unconscious.

Butler explicates the theme of self-confrontation when he suggests to Julian that one feels one should see one's self in the model. The theory he poses on the care one would take if one had such a "dream toy" made invites psychic correlation: "It would almost be taken for granted—one would think—that if a person or a person's surrogate went to the trouble, *and* expense, of having such a dream toy made, that the person *would* have it sealed, so that there'd be no dust." "Dream toy" becomes a significant word choice here when considered in terms of the subconscious. Julian remarks as he gazes into it, "it seemed so . . . continual"; and in response to Butler's comment that the house is enormous he replies, "Endless!" Significantly, in both dimensions, the house has many rooms, as Miss Alice's *non sequitur* points out: "I . . . am a very beautiful woman. . . . And a very rich one. . . . And I live here, in all these rooms." Throughout the play, other references to rooms, divisions, and partitions—the asylum to which Julian committed himself was "deep inland" and had "buildings, or floors of buildings"—bolster the mind imagery. The phrenological head is an obvious symbol.

As I've already suggested, it becomes clear early in the play that Julian's expressed intentions are belied by the unconscious drives which motivate them. The fantasies and hallucinations he divulges betray the libidinous forces threatening his conscious self-concept. In his scenes with Miss Alice, Julian is always the one to initiate an atmosphere of high-tensioned eroticism by relating a past fantasy. (Act 2, scene 3 is surely the best example of this.)

Julian sublimates his sexual drives into a desire to serve and constructs a persona of himself as martyr, refusing to accept that any self-actualization must be channeled into a role which serves his human needs one way or another. In other words, Julian's image of himself as martyr does not eliminate or even substitute for his other needs; it simply displaces them. This repression accounts for the perverse eroticism which fills the stage each time Julian divulges his fantasies. According to C. G. Jung, the ideal relationship of the unconscious to the conscious is compensatory, with the one balancing the extremes of the other. The more repressed the unconscious tendencies— the more, in Julian's case, the sexual needs are denied—the less displaced and the more primitive, even distorted, these tendencies become. The stronger his desires make themselves felt to Julian as doubts or temptations (since the effects of the unconscious will always present themselves as forces outside the person), the more his conscious attitude takes on an extreme, rigid position to compensate. In turn, the unconscious drives become even more exaggerated and grotesque in a continuously vicious cycle. What might have been the healthy expression of his sexuality has become for Julian violent, distorted, and pathological.

Julian's desire for martyrdom, then, is anything but a healthy expression of his faith. It is, rather, an obsessive, fanatical drive to counteract the threat from his unconscious. He is *obsessed* with martyrdom. We might also see this obsession as an impulse toward self-destruction brought on by the tension between his conflicting desires, as well as an unrealized longing for punishment for his transgressions, unconscious though they be. But Albee is hardly offering us any profound insight when he suggests that religious fanaticism if often based upon sexual repression. If his play sought only to uncover Julian as a fraud at the end, after having uncovered institutional religion as a fraud right from the start, *Tiny Alice* would simply be a social statement against all the spiritual trappings, even the most strenuous, with which we surround ourselves. There is certainly that statement made in the play, but it is not the central issue. For one thing, unlike Soeur Jeanne des Anges in John Whiting's *The Devils*, Julian is far too attractive a character. Some critics have suggested that he is, in fact, the most appealing of Albee's protagonists. He is sincerely confused in regard to this area of his life, but in other respects he is open, intelligent, flexible, genuinely simple, and, unlike his Cardinal, without conscious ulterior motives.

And Julian, like George in *Who's Afraid of Virginia Woolf?* and Jerry in *The Zoo Story*, is an outsider, belonging wholeheartedly neither to the traditional hierarchical church, which uses God for its own gains, nor to the secular world, which has long since substituted money and technology for God. His title, lay brother, typifies his situation: "You are of the cloth but have not taken it" as Butler puts it. Because, like Jerry and George, his sensibility precludes his place within traditional structures, Julian is set apart as a modern hero, who, in Jung's words, "has become 'un-historical' in the deepest sense and has estranged himself from the mass of men who live entirely within the bounds of tradition." We find him isolated and at a crossroads: either he must block out the outside world completely and return to the asylum, or he must discard his personal illusions, accept and understand himself, and acknowledge that, again to quote Jung, he "has come to the very edge of the world, leaving behind him all that has been discarded and outgrown, and . . . he stands before the Nothing out of which All may grow."

Therefore, it is difficult to accept that the main motive of the tempters in *Tiny Alice* is to uncover Julian's weaknesses and undermine his good intentions simply to punish him with abandonment and death. If it is necessary for Julian to recognize and discard the fictions he has clung to, as it was for George and Martha to discard their fictional son, we might question whether his possibility for new light and understanding should be any less than theirs. And, if these unconscious motives are uncovered, leaving a more balanced Julian, can we accept that he is betrayed and punished for these unless we accept his own original, distorted definition of his "sins"?

The questions turn on the meaning of Alice and the significance of Julian's acceptance of her. The first part of the play, in which Julian's personal unconscious does become integrated, is only a first or preparatory step, leading to some understanding of even greater, deeper consequence. What this is can be understood in part by viewing *Tiny Alice* not in the context of realistic, ironic tragedy, but within the genre of allegorical romance. Several signs in the play point in this direction.

Northrop Frye states that "in romance the chracters are still largely dream characters" and that they function as "expressions of emotional attachments, whether of wish-fulfillment or of repugnance." The very first word we hear Julian utter, "Extraordinary," in the light of Frye's definition is very apt. From the moment he enters Miss Alice's house there is a sense that he has entered a dreamlike or extra-ordinary world, where commonsense logic will not apply. The characters who people that world are, by their very names, embodiments of ideas, concepts, or split-off parts of Julian's own psyche, on one level at least. Lawyer, for instance, is the prototype of everything repugnant and reductive, Julian's Shadow or dark side as it were, and critics who accept his commentary as a key to understanding the play are hearing only one bias.

Julian's mission contains the obvious allegorical overtones of the life-cycle quest: the accomplishment of a task to achieve a treasure, represented by the money Miss Alice promises to the church. In traditional mythological format, the hero is sent on a task or journey by a divine superior, a role into which the Cardinal fits nicely. Part of his reward is the winning of a bride, whom he takes from the hands of a previous, older lover; the hero, though he must die, is exalted at the end. According to Frye, the quest has three stages: "the stage of the perilous journey and the preliminary minor adventures; the crucial struggle, usually some kind of battle in which either the hero or his foe, or both, must die; and the exaltation of the hero."

From the beginning of act 2, it becomes very clear that little but open hostility exists between Lawyer (the evil ogre) and Miss Alice: lustful pursuit on the part of the one, revulsion and evasion on the part of the other. Lawyer makes such little effort to conceal his tremendous hatred of his successor that Butler can easily observe, "I've noticed, you've let your feelings loose lately; too much: possessiveness, jealousy." Julian himself is fully cognizant of the rivalry, as his accusation to Miss Alice attests: "You have allowed that . . . that *man*, your . . . your lover, to . . . ridicule me. You have *permitted* it. . . . You have allowed him to abuse me, my position, his, the Church; you have tolerated it, and *smiled*."

To quote Frye once again, apropos of Miss Alice:

> This bride-figure is ambiguous: her psychological connection with the mother in an Oedipus fantasy is more insistent than in comedy. She is often to be found in a perilous, forbidden, or tabooed place . . . and she is, of course, often rescued from the unwelcome embraces of another and generally older male, or from giants or bandits or other usurpers.

The tension between Lawyer and Julian reflects the son-father rivalry for the mother. Miss Alice does, in fact, treat Julian as a favored child, referring to him as "my little Julian" and "little recluse." The three characters' interaction as hero/rescuer, bride, and ogre is structured upon the son, mother, father psychological triad in which the child perceives his father as a rival hurting his mother who must be rescued.

That is one level on which the quest motif operates in *Tiny Alice*. On another level, Miss Alice herself is the temptress, and as mother-figure she personifies the most formidable taboo. Julian articulates his instinctive dread of what she represents toward the end of act 2: "WHY AM I BEING TESTED! . . . And why am I being tempted? By luxury, by ease, by . . . content . . . by things I do not care to discuss."

The quest for the treasure is the more generalized version of Julian's specific or personal lifetime preoccupation: the search for the Father, in his terms, God. Within Miss Alice's house his dual purposes converge. He realizes only intuitively at this point that the latter is the search for his Self, a fact implicit in his declaration, "My faith and my sanity . . . they are one and the same."

The motif of the search for the Self brings us, finally, to the last and most elusive level of Albee's play. If the house is the symbol of Julian's unconscious (as well as a female archetype), and Alice lives there, then Alice must be the personification of something within Julian which he must confront. That something can be explored through the Jungian theory of the anima, the female principle existing inside all men.

The anima first appears as an image in a man's mind of the nuturing, all-embracing, protecting mother (but it includes other archetypal images as well, such as the virgin, the temptress, the witch, and the spiritual guide).

It is not clear from where this image arises for it does not come from the real mother. Jung attributed it to the collective unconscious, present *a priori* in a person's mind; while other psychological studies do not accept this completely, they do concede, in the words of Maud Bodkin, that "where forms are assimilated from the environment upon slight contact only, predisposing factors must exist in mind and brain."

In his infantile or immature state, the man will cling to this first image of the mother, his unconscious desire for what Jung calls "the enveloping, embracing, and devouring element." He projects this desire first onto his real mother and later onto the substitute mother, that is, the wife or lover. Seen in this context, Miss Alice is Julian's projection of part of his Anima or his desire, in Jungian terminology, to be caught, sucked in, enveloped, and devoured. This is easily supported from the play by the numerous images of envelopment, for instance, Miss Alice's quote from D. H. Lawrence's "Love on the Farm":

> And down his mouth comes on my mouth! and down
> His bright dark eyes over me . . .
> . . . his lips meet mine, and a flood
> Of sweet fire sweeps across me, so I drown
> Against him, die and find death good!

In Julian's fantasies of martyrdom he sees himself devoured by a lion and after a graphic description he concludes: "And as the fangs sank in, the great tongue on my cheek and eye, the splitting of the bone, and the *blood* . . . just before the great sound, the coming dark and the silence. I could . . . experience it all. And was . . . *engulfed*." When Julian finally comes to Miss Alice in act 2, scene 3, the stage directions indicate that she opens her gown like great wings unfurling and "Julian utters a sort of dying cry and moves, his arms in front of him, to Miss Alice; when he reaches her, she *enfolds* him in her great wings." And, of course, in the final scene the darkness moves out of the model house, surrounds Julian as a presence and, again to quote Albee's directions, "his eyes, his head move to all areas of the room, noticing his *engulfment*." (All emphases, except the first, mine.)

Mother Church, to which Julian's loyalties lie before he relinquishes them to Miss Alice, is also an archetypal anima—the female counterpart to Christ, the male animus. We might recollect, too, that Julian's memory of his first sexual experience which "did or did not happen" involved a woman who believed herself to be yet another female archetype: the Virgin Mary, mother of God.

When Miss Alice appears in act 1, scene 3 as, in Albee's directions, a "withered crone, her hair gray and white and matted," bent and moving with two canes, and speaks "with a cracked and ancient voice," this is more than simply an indication that in this play things will not be as they seem, though it certainly is that. The disguise is also a sign, from the outset, that she is playing a role—the donning of a mask transforms the wearer into an archetypal image—a role with mythic significance. In this case, she is the projection of another aspect of the anima of Julian's psyche: the terrible mother, which appears in archetypal dream imagery as a witch or crone. The duality between the good mother and the terible mother is explained best by a quotation from Ruth L. Munroe regarding Jungian theory:

> For the infant the mother is the major image, regardless of the sex of the child, and the mother remains the symbol of bliss, repose, comfort, and total passivity, the source of life. But a duality is apparent in the definition. Life is not passive. The child must go forth into the real world. So while the man retains a nostalgia for the Eternal Mother . . . he must also leave the Mother. The Good Mother of his deepest dreams is also the Terrible Mother . . . within the person's own psyche.
> [*Schools of Psychoanalytic Thought: An Exposition, Critique, and Attempt at Integration*]

The terrible mother is associated with death and the dark side of life a man must accept in order to live actively. Therefore, when Miss Alice appears to Julian first as a crone this is a message to him from his own psyche that, in order to find what he is looking for, he must first leave the safety of his secluded world, the confines of Mother Church. In light of this, the exchange between Julian and Miss Alice after she has removed the mask makes more sense than it otherwise would:

MISS ALICE: Oh, indulge us, please.
JULIAN: Well, of course, it would be my pleasure . . . but, considering the importance of our meeting . . .
MISS ALICE: Exactly. Considering the importance of our meeting.
JULIAN: A . . . a test for me.

Julian comes very close to a conscious awareness of the meaning of the terrible mother when he describes his meeting with her as a test. He will not arrive at full consciousness of everything that is happening to him, however, until the very end of the play. These events and the people who act within them are simply signals from his unconscious, similar to the symbols of dreams,

revealing a great deal of what his conscious self cannot immediately comprehend. The extent to which this is true adds weight to the association
frequently made between the title of the play and the wonderland of Lewis
Carroll's Alice. It may be to her function as a dream symbol (which is
experienced but not always understood) that Miss Alice refers when she says
early in the play, "It may be I am . . . noticeable, but almost never identified."

Though Julian is obviously fascinated and enticed by Miss Alice, this
alone would not provide sufficient incentive for his renunciation of the safety
of Mother Church. Miss Alice must lure him out of that world and into a
dynamic participation in life. In her primary role of temptress, she does this
by being to him still another projection of his desire for "the protecting,
nourishing, charmed circle of the mother." He succumbs to this illusion
when he comes to her uttering "a sort of dying cry" and she enfolds him in
her wings. This is a point of initiation for Julian, necessitating the loss of
innocence (Albee, in an interview appearing in the April 1965 issue of The
Atlantic Monthly, referred to Julian as an innocent); he undergoes a symbolic
death and an entrance into experience resulting in the sacrifice of rigidly
idealistic (and, by implication, immature) beliefs. Thus, as the hero, Julian
experiences a kind of initial rebirth into a more autonomous individualism,
enabling him to continue on his quest to penetrate the mysteries of life and
death. A definition from Jung further explicates Miss Alice's role: "the se-
ductress . . . draws him into life with her Maya [Illusion personified as a
celestial maiden]—and not only into life's reasonable and useful aspects, but
into its frightful *paradoxes* and *ambivalence* where good and evil, success and
ruin, hope and despair counterbalance one another."

That Julian has, in fact, progressed in his journey and shed his limiting
and self-protecting beliefs is suggested by his words to the Cardinal in the
scene following his marriage to Miss Alice:

> But then I judge it is God's doing, this . . . wrenching of my life
> from one light to another . . . though not losing God's light,
> joining it with . . . my new. I can't tell you, the . . . radiance,
> humming, and the witchcraft, I think it must be, the ecstasy of
> this light, as *God's* exactly; . . . the blessed wonder of service with
> a renewing, not an ending joy—that joy I thought possible only
> through martyrdom.

Julian intuits that his entrance into life has had something to do with witch-
craft. Though he is focusing on the bright side (which is real), he senses that
there is a dark side as well (also real). His first experience of leaving the
mother's womblike safety is abandonment. In fact, at the opening of that

same scene we see Julian, the bridegroom, confused and anxious as to why everyone, including his new wife, has left him on his wedding day. One of the first things he says is, "I feel quite *lost*," and a little later, "There I was . . . one moment married, flooded with white, and . . . then . . . the next, alone. Quite alone. . . ." Entering the continuum of life he begins to experience the "frightful paradoxes" Jung speaks of, where light and dark, the Apollonian and the Dionysian, expansion and diminution exist side by side.

Miss Alice seems to be Julian's betrayer by initiating him into that world, but he must take that necessary step toward the goal he has set for himself, a goal he cannot reach without *conscious* acceptance (in the final scene) of everything happening to him so far in his unconscious. His only alternative is complete withdrawal from the world; that is, total surrender to his unconscious, the substitution of hallucination for reality. Lawyer and Butler refer to these two alternatives when they speak of Julian in act 2, scene 2 as "walking on the edge of an abyss, but . . . balancing. Can be pushed . . . over, back to the asylums. Or over . . . to the Truth." This Truth will come with the integration of the conscious and the unconscious, with the attainment of the masculine principle to balance the feminine, and with the acceptance of the ambiguities, paradoxes, and limitations which will become recognizable. In this sense, it must be remembered that Miss Alice is the projection of Julian's own anima seeking this balance. And even when, in Act 3, he is lost and abandoned after his marriage, he has not forsaken his quest. The pain of "the reality of things" is so great, however, that Julian's ego resists it to the point where he almost opts for insanity: "I . . . cannot . . . accept . . . this. . . . No, no, I will . . . I will go *back*! I will . . . go *back* to it. To . . . to . . . I will go back to the asylum."

According to Jung, if the conscious and the unconscious become too split, as in the case of Julian, a tension arises, and the functions of the anima in a man and the animus in a woman, "harmless till then, confront the conscious mind in personified form and behave rather like systems split off from the personality, or like part souls." It must be made very clear, I think, that on one level Lawyer, Miss Alice, and Butler function as full, three-dimensional characters with independent motivations and psychologies. But on another level, they are projections of Julian's mind. It is because of this dual function that their roles and rhetoric become so confusing.

If, in the case of Julian, the Anima can be withdrawn from projections, these projections can be integrated into consciousness. Thus, to a certain extent, the anima represents a *function* which filters the collective unconscious through to the conscious mind. Alluding to this function, Miss Alice attempts to explain to Julian, "I have tried to be . . . *her*. No; I have tried to be . . .

what I thought she might, what might make you happy, what you might use, as a . . . what?" and later, "accept what's real. I am the . . . illusion"; to which Lawyer refers when he says, "We are surrogates; *our* task is done now." As functionaries of Julian's psyche, Lawyer's, Butler's, and Miss Alice's tasks are done as they bring him to the point of consciousness, in which they can no longer be personified for him by projections, and so in a sense must abandon him. As archetypal symbols, however, they function beyond Julian's psyche in the realm of a collective unconscious. Therefore, they remain autonomous even after he has integrated them into his ego ("On . . . and on . . . we go"). Becauses of this, Lawyer declares, "You have brought us to the end of our service here. We go on; you stay." The indications are that they will continue to act the same roles within other circumstances.

Like Sophocles' Oedipus, Julian had been on a search for the truth; like Oedipus who questioned everyone, Julian was sent to Miss Alice's house to take care of "a few questions and answers"; and like Oedipus, Julian had not bargained for the outcome that truth is painful, that it brings with it the recognition of unconscious forces and existential alienation, and that it leads ultimately to self-confrontation. His anger toward, and rejection of, Miss Alice's protective gesture in the last act of *Tiny Alice* underscores the dawning of his understanding of autonomy and acceptance of responsibility: "It is what I have wanted, have insisted on. Have nagged . . . for."

Albee has insisted that though "The sound of heartbeats and heavy breathing as the doors open have widely been misinterpreted as being those of an increasingly terrified Julian . . . they are meant to belong to whatever comes through the door." Alice is the abstraction of the anima which exists in the most sublimated realm of Julian's unconscious—his archetypal or collective unconscious. In recognizing *her*, Julian finds her counterpart, the animus, or the God for which he has been searching; and consequently he comes to possess himself.

The animus or logos representing the male aspect of spirit and intellect, and the anima or eros representing the female or earth mother are, as Jung tells us, godlike because of the great psychic energy they produce:

> Both of them are unconscious powers, "gods" in fact, as the ancient world quite rightly conceived them to be. To call them by this name is to give them that central position in the scale of psychological values which has always been theirs whether consciously acknowledged or not; for their power grows in proportion to the degree that they remain unconscious.

In accepting them both, Julian has reached his epiphany which, according to Northrop Frye, is:

> the symbolic presentation of the point at which the undisplaced apocalyptic world and the cyclical world of nature come into alignment. . . . Its most common settings are the mountain-top, the island, the tower, the lighthouse, and the ladder or staircase. Folk tales and mythologies are full of stories of an original connection between heaven or the sun and earth. . . . The movement from one world to the other may be symbolized by the golden fire that descends from the sun . . . and by its human response, the fire kindled on the sacrificial altar.

The setting for Julian is up against the model house, the alter of Alice, but it is interesting that Albee originally intended him to be locked in an attic closet (corresponding more closely to Frye's tower or ladder), an idea he had to forego for the sake of dramatic effect. The movement of the world of nature (Alice) into the world of the spirit (God) comes in the form of the light descending through the rooms of the model house into the room Julian occupies (Frye's golden fire descending from the sun). Julian is the human response on the sacrificial altar.

Through a modern rite of initiation Julian comes, at last, to achieve the integration he sought. What the drama depicts, finally, is a birth-rebirth ritual in which he is first outfitted in ritual robes (in his case, a business suit), shot with a pistol (phallic symbol of fertility), and united with the earth mother who destroys in order to immortalize. In an impressive feat of dramatic compression, the scene of his death, with heartbeats and ensuing darkness, carries unmistakable overtones of a birth—expulsion from the womb. The modern audience may well remain impervious, however, to the suggestion of spiritual rebirth for Julian since, as Jung argues in his essay "Freud and Jung," our civilization has by and large forgotten the meaning of divine procreation and tends to overlook the possibility that incestuous longings go back past the desire for the temporal father and mother to a primal desire for unity with the spirit and with nature.

Perhaps in this play, in which Albee must surely have been working out of his own unconscious, his contention that the use of the unconscious is twentieth-century theatre's most interesting development comes most fully to bear. The psychological processes dissected here occur simultaneously in the play so that the overall effect contributes to its most fascinating element: the capacity to re-create the atmosphere of the dream. Thus, it is haunting and disturbing despite its resistance to discursive logic.

Like many of Albee's plays, the effect of the ending of *Tiny Alice* is one of suspended motion; there is a sense of resolution but it remains intangible. Julian's epiphany is as elusive as the elation Jerry experiences right before his death in *The Zoo Story:* a bright flash of light before what remains, for us, darkness. Both characters, at their deaths, take the full implication of their visions with them, leaving the audience to ponder, finally, the persistent sense of mystery which remains.

JULIAN N. WASSERMAN

The Idea of Language in the Plays of Edward Albee

In response to an interviewer's question concerning the supposed lack of "realism" in his work, Edward Albee noted the implicit contradiction between the nature of drama as imitation, in the Aristotelian sense, and the expectation of realism on the part of a play's audience. The importance of this argument is that such a recognition goes far beyond the aesthetics of drama and touches upon the symbolic, that is imitative, nature of language— a problem that is frequently at the thematic heart of Albee's works. Indeed, the common thread that runs through many of his seemingly diverse plays is his characters' oft-stated concern with language and, in particular, the failures annd limitations of the linguistic medium. For Albee, language is the medium or meeting ground which exists between the interior and exterior worlds of the speaker and the listener. As a playwright, he seems most interested in the function of language as a means of translating ideas into actions and in the role of language as mediator where a word, like a play, is an imitation which is a wholly independent sign, distinct and separate from that which it represents. As such, a word, like any piece of drama, is neither a pure idea of an action or event nor the event itself. In essence, the naming done by the semanticist and the storytelling practiced by the playwright are, for Albee, congruent if not identical actions.

The problematical nature of language is succinctly set forth in *Seascape* during an argument between Charlie and Nancy in the opening scene of the play. The practical onset of the debate is Charlie's use of the past rather

From *Edward Albee: An Interview And Essays.* © 1983 by The University of St. Thomas.

than present perfect tense, and as so often happens in the works of Albee, the linguistic bartering over a particular term quickly evolves into a more general and abstract debate over the nature and function of language:

NANCY: Do you know what I'm *saying?*

CHARLIE: *You're throwing it up to me; you're telling me I've had*
    a . . .

NANCY: *No-no-no! I'm saying what you said, what you told me.* You
    told me, you said to me, "You've had a good life."

CHARLIE: *(Annoyed.)* Well, you have! You *have* had!

NANCY: *(She, too.)* Yes! Have *had!* What *about* that!

CHARLIE: What about it!

NANCY: *Am* not *having. (Waits for reaction; gets none)* Am not
    having? Am not *having* a good life?

CHARLIE: Well, of *course!*

NANCY: Then why say had? Why put it that way?

CHARLIE: It's a way of speaking!

NANCY: No! It's a way of thinking! *I* know the language and I
    know *you.* You're not careless with it, or didn't used to be.
    Why *not* go to those places in the desert and let our heads
    deflate, if it's all in the past? Why not just *do* that?

CHARLIE: It was a way of speaking.

NANCY: Dear God, we're *here.* We've served out time, Charlie
    and there's nothing telling us to do *that,* or any
    conditional; not any more. Well, there's the arthritis in my
    wrist, of course, and the eyes have known a better season,
    and there's always the cancer or a heart attack to think
    about if we're bored, but besides all these things . . . what
    is there?

CHARLIE: *(Somewhere triste.)* You're at it again.

NANCY: I am! Words are lies; they *can* be, and you *use* them,
    but I know what's in your gut. I *told* you, didn't I?

The problem, then, is that language, while it is the figurative medium through which Charlie is expressing the feelings in his "gut," is merely a symbol for those feelings and may, by nature, serve to obscure rather than to reveal them. As Nancy notes, her understanding of Charlie's meaning is intuitive rather than linguistic and is based first on her knowledge of Charlie and, second, on her understanding of the nature of language. Furthermore, an important part of the argument out of which these linguistic considerations arise is devoted to Charlie's and Nancy's discussion of their sexual fantasies, or as Nancy terms it, the problem of "when the real and the figurative come together." Remarkably, the discussion of these sexual imaginings which Nancy describes as "the sad fantasies, the substitutions, the thoughts we have" culminates in Nancy's discovery that Charlie's fantasy was to "pretend that I was me," thus again presenting the attempt to join the intangible product of the inner man with that which is experienced in the world of phenomena. Described in slightly different—though still in a combination of philosophical, linguistic, and sexual terms—the same desire is expressed by The Man in *Listening:* "Odd, in retrospect: it's such a thing we all want— though we seldom admit it, and when we *do*, only part; we all wish to devour ourselves, enter ourselves, be the subject and the object all at once; we all love ourselves and wish we could." The goal is to make subject and object, idea and form, identical, and the pronouncement is immediately followed by a short interval of linguistic "bargaining" over The Man's use of the word "take."

Furthermore, the conversation containing sexual fantasies which appears at the beginning of *Seascape* contains a likewise significant discussion in which Charlie and Nancy compare the difference between their memories of days past and their perceptions of their less pleasant present. Finally, the opening dialogue contains Nancy's suggestion that Charlie attempt to recapture those days, or make memory and fact one, by re-enacting his childhood act of holding stones and sinking to the bottom of the sea in order to escape, if only for a moment, the chaos of the world above. This, of course, all serves as a prelude to the face to face confrontation between the humans and their reptilian counterparts. As the dialogue between the beings from, in their own words, two different dimensions might suggest, the conjunction between the real and the ideal is clearly the central theme of the play.

As the lines from *Listening* suggest, the playwright's concern with the relationship between idea and actuality is certainly not limited to *Seascape*. The same nominalistic exploration is most elaborately set forth in the abstract in *Tiny Alice* with its butler named "Butler," a symbolic precursor of the joining of the real and the figurative in Charlie's sexual fantasies. The originally intended title of the earlier play, "Substitute Speaker," and its use of Alice as a substitute or proxy for the "Abstract" in the marriage to Julian further suggest a connection with the "substitutions" of which Nancy speaks in the discussion of fantasy. The same theme is no less forcefully, though a good deal less obliquely, presented in the battle over "Truth and Illusion" in *Who's Afraid of Virginia Woolf?*. It is there that the illusionary is made real in the imaginary son and that the real is made illusion in George's "auto- biographical" novel. Thus while Albee has enjoyed a reputation as an innovator whose constant experimentation has, to some, robbed his work of a clear and consistent stylistic voice, his plays have for the most part maintained a consistency of thematic concern. Significantly, most of those concerns will be seen to be the natural outgrowths or even elaborations of the material of his first play.

In *The Zoo Story*, the theme of the disparity between idea and experience is again presented in regard to sexual fantasy as is seen in Jerry's description of the pornographic playing cards: "What I wanted to get at is the value difference between pornographic playing cards when you're older. It's that when you're a kid you use the cards as a substitute for a real experience, and when you're older you use real experience as a substitute for the fantasy." What is important here is that, whether one begins with ideas and moves toward experience or whether one moves in the opposite direction, a disparity always remains. The recognition of that disparity is the essential content of Jerry's vision. Whether the process begins with either the idea or the object, one must inevitably be, in Nancy's terms, a "substitution" for the other and therefore different in actual identity. That is why the dialogue between Charlie, Nancy, and their reptilian counterparts must inevitably fail. No matter that they are joined by a verb; subject can never be co-incidental with objects, to borrow the terminology of The Man from *Listening*, no matter how much we may wish it. As with *Seascape*, the bulk of Albee's first play comes to be an elaboration of this vision whose content is the necessary failure of communication. To be sure, the action of *The Zoo Story* might be described as the process of translation of Jerry's death fantasy into action, just as the presence of the sea lizards in *Seascape* is the externalizing of objectification of the debate between Charlie and Nancy. It is important, however, to emphasize that the phenomenalization of Jerry's fantasy is brought about through language and that Peter is, significantly enough, a publisher by profession. Indeed, the process is overtly linguistic. It is the ongoing process of definition. The play reaches its climax over the argument as to whether or not Peter is a "vegetable." In the linguistic bargaining which takes place, Peter is called upon to take action in order to deny the validity of the name which has been apllied to him. When in the final twist, Peter proves himself not to be a "vegetable" but rather an "animal," society, at large, is thereby defined as a "zoo," and it is this secret definition, a linguistic riddle of identity, that is the mystery which is at the heart of the play. The play as a whole might, then, well be taken as a type of extended definition. This idea of drama as linguistic process is likewise clearly seen in the playwright's *Counting the Ways*, which serves as little more than an extended definition of love. Remembering that Albee has throughout his career insisted that his writing begins with the creation of characters and then progresses to placing those characters in particular situations, the playwright's work, as has just been seen in *The Zoo Story*, may be seen as unfolding revelations of character and identity. Keeping in mind Elizabeth's pronouncement in *The Lady from Dubuque:* "In the outskirts of Dubuque . . . I learned—though I doubt I knew I was learning it—that all of the values were relative save one . . . Who am I? All the rest is semantics—liberty, dignity, possession," those exercises seem to be essentially semantic in nature.

While this preoccupation with the process of definition is not always as center stage as it is in *Counting the Ways*, it is without exception present in Albee's work. Whether in the more naturalistic dialogue of *Virginia Woolf* or in the seeming collection of non-sequiturs of *Listening*, a major topic of conversation—and admittedly there is a great deal more of talking than of action in Albee's plays—is language and, in particular, semantics. In its most absurdist form, this preoccupation is present in the wonderfully comic tale of the confrontation between Mommy and Mrs. Barker over the color of their hats in *The American Dream*, a work which Albee has described as a play about failed communication. The same play also contains such semantic considerations as the difference between a "house" and an "apartment" or between an "enema bag" and an "enema bottle" as well as a wealth of word plays on such words as "badger" and "bumble/bundle." Each of Albee's plays has a host of similar verbal offerings. *Seascape*, because it deals so directly with the problem of language, again provides an excellent example of the relativity of definition through its comic debate between Charlie and Leslie, the male lizard, over the proper name for the front arm/leg. In a semantic exercise which is much in keeping with the debate over the color of Mommy's hat, Charlie begins,

CHARLIE: When we meet we . . . take each other's hands, or
    whatever, and we . . . touch.
NANCY: . . . Let's greet each other properly, all right? *(Extends
    her hand again.)* I give you my hand, and you give me your
    . . . what *is* that? What is that called?
LESLIE: What?
NANCY: *(Indicating Leslie's right arm.)* That there.
LESLIE: It's called a leg, of course.
NANCY: Oh. Well, we call this an arm.
LESLIE: You have four arms, I see.
CHARLIE: No; she has two arms. *(Tiny pause.)* And two legs.
SARAH: *(Moves closer to examine Nancy with Leslie.)* And which are
    the legs?
NANCY: These here. And these are the arms.

LESLIE: *(A little on his guard.)* Why do you differentiate?
NANCY: Why do we differentiate, Charlie?
CHARLIE: *(Quietly hysterical.)* Because they're the ones with the
    hands on the ends of them.
NANCY: *(To Leslie.)* Yes.
SARAH: *(As Leslie glances suspiciously at Charlie.)* Go on, Leslie; do
    what Nancy wants you to do. *(To Nancy.)* What is it
    called?
NANCY: Shaking hands.
CHARLIE: Or legs.

This verbal bartering continues until the inevitable result is achieved. The
sea lizard, in a fashion highly reminiscent of Peter's anger at being called a
"vegetable," takes umbrage at being termed a "fish." It would seem, then,
that the major thrust of *Seascape* may be summed up in Leslie's annoyed
response to Charlie's and Nancy's inability to define the human concepts of
love and emotion: "We may, or we may not, but we'll never know unless
you define your terms. Honestly, the imprecision! You're so thoughtless!"
For his part, Charlie at a subsequent moment retorts in kind as he demands
of Nancy, "What *standards* are you using? How would *you* know?" The point
of these interchanges is that the existential situation of man is that he must,
by the nature of his being, attempt to define his terms and standards, although
he is also, by nature, incapable of doing so. Given the playwright's interest
in Japanese *Noh* drama as well as Charlie's use of the Rinzai Zen Koan, "What
is the sound of one hand clapping?" it would appear that Albee's concept of
language is essentially Zen in nature. That is, language as a temporal creation
is rooted in the phenomenal while the ideas which it attempts to convey find
their source in the ontological. The result of this paradox is that definitions
are futile attempts to cast the infinite in the garb of the finite and are of
necessity doomed to failure. Such exercises ultimately obscure more than
they reveal because of a mistaken notion of their completeness and an ill-
placed faith in their ability to capture completely the essence of the subject
being defined. Hence, all of the semantic debates, whether over the proper
names of colors or anatomical features, are always unresolvable because, by
presenting only partial or relative truths, language is a means by which one
may, in the playwright's own words, go to "great lengths to avoid communication. . . . Talk in order not to have to listen."

   In all of the naming contests which occur throughout his plays, what
exists is for the most part a series of futile semantic debates in which each
side insists on judging and defining according to its own perceptive standards.
As George wryly tells Nick in *Virginia Woolf*, "Every definition has its

boundaries, eh?" That definitions are thus implicitly faulty is seen in Oscar's use of the qualifier "as definitions go" in *The Lady from Dubuque*. To be sure, the implicit doubt of the validity of definitions is the key to the play as a whole. After all, the turning point of the play is the miraculous appearance of Elizabeth, the woman who claims to be Jo's mother. In its abruptness, the appearance of Oscar and Elizabeth is much like that of Leslie and Sarah, the sea lizards. Furthermore, as with the reptiles, their appearance seems to be an objectification of what has previously been presented only in the abstract, for the audience has already been given an indirect description of Jo's mother. The dramatic tension comes from the fact that Elizabeth, in the words of Lucinda, is simply "not what [she] imagined" and is completely unknown to Sam, Jo's husband. In other words, the objectification, as with the symbolic acts of both language and drama, conforms to neither the expected nor the known. The play, like so many others by Albee, ends with the audience left in doubt about the meaning of its title. If Elizabeth is aptly described by the title/name "The Lady from Dubuque," then she is, in fact, not Jo's mother since the latter lives in New Jersey. The situation is much like that of *Tiny Alice* where the audience must decide whether to apply the name of the play to the visible onstage character or the offstage abstraction. In each case, the title is a name and as such a definition which is part of each and applies fully to neither with the result that the audience is left with the dilemma of how and when to apply the titular definition.

Albee's insistence on the relativity of words seems to rely heavily on the standard linguistic assertion that each speech act derives its meaning from three sources: the meaning of the word in the mind of the speaker, the meaning of the word in the mind of the listener, and, most importantly, the generally accepted meaning of the word in the speech community of which both speaker and listener are members. As has already been seen, Albee's plays can be viewed as his examinations of these complex relationships. The plays regularly take members from different speech communities, dimensions, worlds, or societies and present their attempts at forging or working out a new, common vocabulary. Even when speakers come from the same speech communities, they of necessity spend most of their time attempting to explain their private meanings. However, the lack of a common language can also be fostered in order to create an impassable gulf between characters. Yam in *Fam and Yam: An Imaginary Interview* reassures Fam in regard to a certain critic by saying, ". . . but after all, you and a man like that just don't talk the same language." Language is thus used both to include and exclude. Yam uses language to establish a communal bond between himself and Fam and at the same time to separate Fam from the community of critics.

The same linguistic exclusion is readily apparent in *Virginia Woolf*. When asked if he and Martha have any children, George replies to Nick, "That's for me to know and you to find out." It is "finding out" or the solving of the riddle that is, within the play, the process of definition. It is only when Nick discovers that the child whom he assumed to be real is, in fact, the product of his hosts' imaginations that even a rudimentary understanding of the dialogue can begin. It is the final revelation that assumed fact is, in reality, fiction which gives all of the previous language its meaning. Before this final revelation, Martha has already berated Nick for his limited understanding:

> You always deal in appearances? . . . you don't see anything, do
> you? You see everything but the goddamn mind; you see all the
> little specks and crap, but you don't see what goes on, do you?

Throughout the play, Nick deals only in the concrete while George and Martha speak the language of abstraction. True communication between Nick and his hosts is impossible, so despite the fact that Nick tells George, "I'll play the charades like you've got 'em set up. . . . I'll play in your language. . . . I'll be what you say I am," Nick is doomed to failure not merely because he is not as skillful as George at word play but because he has no understanding of either the vocabulary or the rules by which the linguistic game is played, for as George makes clear at the end of the play, the rules are definite and absolute, and there is a penalty to be exacted for their violation.

Despite the fact that it is their immediate presence which acts as the catalyst for the "fun and games" which are acted out before them, Nick and Honey are, in essence, passive observers. When they enter the action at all, they serve solely as the objects of manipulation, despite any illusions which they may have to the contrary. For the most part, they are mere sounding boards, a convenient direction in which to aim speeches made about subjects in a *patois* which is both unknown and unintelligible at the outset of the play. It is little wonder, then, that there is no real communication between the two couples in the course of the night's action. George and Martha have, between themselves, all of the private, mutually exclusive meanings which they assign to events in their lives as well as a mutually agreed upon vocabulary and an enforceable set of rules for its implementation. This is the source of their togetherness, their comic unity. In contrast, there exists no such bond between either George or Martha and either of their guests. When Nick attempts to converse with George, it is as though the two were attempting to converse in two mutually exclusive tongues without the aid of an interpreter. While George is aware of this fact, Nick is not, and George

refuses to explain or to translate. In their linguistic exclusion from the conversations between George and Martha, Nick and Honey are, themselves,
models or metaphors for the members of the audience, objectified and placed
on stage. Like Nick and Honey, the members of the audience, although the
"cause" or occasion of the night's performance, are placed in the positions
of passive eavesdroppers to the verbal antics of their hosts. The process of
the play is for the audience, as well as for the younger couple on stage, the
gradual understanding of those antics and games and hence inclusion into
the speech community founded by George and Martha. The play, then, is
a linguistic exercise, a teaching of language or at least a forging of a common
language founded on an initial act of exclusion and followed by an initiation
or movement toward inclusion. The comic unity of the play, and Albee has
from the outset stoutly maintained that *Virginia Woolf* is a comedy, is its
movement from perceived disunity of George's and Martha's seeming non-
sequiturs and highly eccentric speech to a perception of the unity or coherence of their speeches as we learn the semantic and lexical rules of their
private tongue. This change in perception takes place when the audience
ceases to be excluded from and instead becomes a part of the speech community of George and Martha. And it is important to note that this change
is a change in the perception of the reality, not in the reality itself. George
was, despite appearances, making "sense" all along. That is, the solving of
the riddle, the catharsis, the "finding out" as George puts it, is a linguistic
and phenomenal rather than an ontological matter. This is, in the last analysis, the same comic action that was the essential structure of Albee's first
play, where the solving of the riddle is the passive observer's ultimate recognition that Jerry's seeming nonsequiturs concerning "the zoo" are not
unintelligible ravings. Jerry's comments to Peter, like those of George to
Nick, make sense and are in fact seen as truthful as soon as one understands
the language in which those "ravings" are cast.

Language, then, can serve as a bridge or medium between speaker and
listener but only when both parties are fully aware of its rules and nature.
When either half of the equation is missing, the result from the linguist's
point of view is not really true language. The point is made by Charlie who
in *Seascape* tells Nancy that "parrots don't talk; parrots imitate." Here the
linguistic principle that thought must precede the speech act is championed.
The parrot does not talk because it does not think. It has no awareness of
the fact that its utterances comprise human words, and most important of
all, it has no understanding of their meanings, either public or private. In
this sense, the parrot is like Nick in *Virginia Woolf* or Sam in *The Lady from
Dubuque* who both find themselves unwilling and even unconscious partici-

pants in a repartee in which they know neither the rules nor the vocabulary. Albee's interest in the epistemological basis of speech is most clearly seen in a brief interchange from *Listening:*

THE GIRL: You don't *listen.*

THE WOMAN: *(As if the Man were not there.)* Well, that may *be.*

THE GIRL: Pay attention, rather, is what you don't do.
  Listen: oh, yes; carefully, to . . . oh, the sound an idea makes . . .

THE WOMAN: . . . a *thought.*

THE GIRL: No; an idea.

THE WOMAN: As it does what?

THE GIRL: *(Thinks about that for a split second.)* Mmmmmm . . . as the chemical thing happens, and then the electric thing, and then the muscle; *that* progression. The response—that almost reflex thing, the movement, when an idea happens. *(A strange little smile.)* That *is* the way the brain works, is it not? The way it functions? Chemical, then electric, then muscle? *(The woman does an "et voilà!" gesture.)*

THE MAN: *(Quiet awe.)* Where does it come from?

THE WOMAN: What?

THE MAN: The . . . all that. Where does it come from?

THE WOMAN: I haven't found out. It all begins right there: she says, "You don't listen." Every time, she says: "You don't listen."

THE MAN: To what!? You don't listen to what!?

THE WOMAN: *(Sotto voce.)* I don't *know* what I don't listen to.

THE MAN: *(Accusatory.)* Yes, and do you care?

THE WOMAN: *(So reasonable.)* I DON'T *know.*

THE MAN: *(Snorting.)* Of course not!

THE WOMAN: *(Quite brusque.)* Defend the overdog once in a while, will you!? At least what you *think* it is. How do you know who's what!?

THE MAN: I don't!

THE WOMAN: All right!

THE MAN: (Shrugs; throws it away.) Get behind that sentence, that's all you have to do. Find out what precedes.

The passage touches upon all the elements necessary for true linguistic communication as it follows the stages of the unconscious genesis of an idea to its establishment in the consciousness of the speaker to its final articulation and reception by a listener. As the title of the play suggests, the final stage is as important as the first. One must, to quote The Girl, not merely listen but also pay attention. A listener, then, is as important to language as a speaker; without a true listener who pays attention, language must out of necessity fail. As Albee has, himself, pointed out in several interviews, Mommy can tell Mrs. Barker, in *The American Dream* to take off her dress rather than her coat because no one in the room is paying any attention to what anyone else is saying. That is why the play is, according to its author, a play about the failure of communication. Significantly, the need for true communication is so great that its failure can result in madness. An important part of the "madness" of The Girl in *Listening* is her resentment over the fact that The Woman really doesn't "Listen." Similarly, Julian, in *Tiny Alice*, equates his own descent into madness with a loss of the ability to hear and comprehend language: "The periods of hallucination would be announced by a ringing in the ears, which produced, or was accompanied by, a loss of hearing. I would hear people's voices from a great distance and through the roaring of . . . surf. And my body would feel light, and not mine, and I would float, not glide."

If speaker and listener are essential to the linguistic process, then one must ask what is the nature of the operation which takes place between the two. To borrow a phrase from The Man in *Listening*, each attempts to "get behind" (that is, understand the generating idea) the sentence or public pronouncement between them. Without the kind of intuition which Nancy claims in regard to understanding what is in Charlie's "gut," one must of necessity rely on indirect means such as symbols or words which are by nature finite compromises for infinite complexities. An example of the kind of linguistic bartering that is necessary although futile is found in the description of the wrapped lunch in *The American Dream:*

> MOMMY: And every day, when I went to school, Grandma used to wrap a box for me, and I used to take it with me to school; and when it was lunchtime, all the little boys and girls used to take out their boxes of lunch, and they weren't wrapped nicely at all, and they used to open them and eat their chicken legs and chocolate cakes; and I used to say, "Oh, look at my lovely lunch box; it's so nicely wrapped it would break my heart to open it." And so, I wouldn't open it.
>
> DADDY: Because it was empty.

> MOMMY: Oh no. Grandma always filled it up, because she
> never ate the dinner she cooked the evening before; she
> gave me all her food for my lunch box the next day. After
> school, I'd take the box back to Grandma, and she'd open
> it and eat the chicken legs and chocolate cake that was
> inside. Grandma used to say, "I love day-old cake." That's
> where the expression day-old cake came from. Grandma
> always ate everything a day late. I used to eat all the other
> little boys' and girls' food at school, because they thought
> my lunch box was empty, and that's why I wouldn't open
> it. They thought I suffered from the sin of pride, and
> since that made them better than me, they were very
> generous.

The point here is that, while there is a seeming common understanding concerning the external appearance of the box, each person believed it to contain something different. In the same fashion, words which seem clear and apparent frequently have individual and sometimes antithetical, private meanings to the characters who use them within the context of the play. Thus, when Grandma in *The American Dream* presents the mysterious boxes around which everyone must negotiate, those boxes are in essence words, and, indeed, Grandma's most consistent complaint throughout the play concerns the way in which everyone speaks to the elderly. Words, then, are to Albee types of decorated boxes sometimes containing wonderful surprises as in the comic debates between Charlie and Leslie, or they can serve as virtual Pandora's boxes as they do in the cases of George and Martha. As Fam says in his interview with Yam, "Words; words . . . They're such a pleasure," and as George notes, "Martha's a devil with language: she really is."

As the case with George and Martha might suggest, the field of semantics is the arena in which the tug of war between reality and fantasy ultimately takes place. Nowhere is this made clearer than in *Tiny Alice*. In that play, many of Albee's concerns with the symbolic nature of language find their expression in the semantic debate over the curious relationship between the house in which Alice resides and the model which it contains. The house, it seems, was originally constructed in England and then disassembled and rebuilt in its present location. The house, therefore, is not by definition an "original" but is, rather, a "replica." Although built of the materials of the original, the replica can no more be the original than a word can be identical to the mental image which it signifies. The replica once again presents the playwright's preoccupation with the translation of ideas, persons, and objects. Translation, however, in these terms implies an absolute alteration of the item translated, for it implies a definite and distinct change from one location or state of being to another. In the midst of the replica stands a "model"—the proportionately correct although scaled down symbol which is derivative, though wholly separate from the original. It should, however, be noted that the model is subject to the vicissitudes which affect the replica and not *vice versa*. This is seen in the fact that while the fire is first noted in the chapel of the model it is, in fact, put out in the chapel of the replica. As in the case of the fire in the chapel, one learns about the house, the replica, by studying the model. If the model is to be exact, it must contain a model, which, in turn, must contain a model. The process must go on *ad infinitum*. The infinite nature of the series of reflective models required to establish the model as an exact duplicate of the replica presents an example of Xeno's paradox concerning the tortoise and the hare. Just as the hare can never in theory overtake the tortoise, so the model can never reach its goal of reduplicating either the replica or the original.

To understand the complex relationship which Albee is suggesting here, it is necessary to turn to a similar set of relationships in the later play, *Listening*, as The Girl describes the mysterious "blue cardboard":

> Yes. Most cardboard is grey . . . or brown, heavier. But blue cardboard is . . . unusual. That would be enough, but if you see blue cardboard, tile blue, love it, want . . . it, and have it . . . then it's special. But—don't interrupt me!—Well, if you want more value from it, from the experience, and take *grey* cardboard, mix your colors and paint it, carefully, blue, to the edges, smooth, then it's not *any* blue cardboard but very special: grey cardboard taken and made blue, self-made, self-made blue—better than grey, better than the other blue, because it's self-done. Very valuable, and even looking at it is a theft; touching it, even to take it to a window to see the smooth lovely color, all blue, is a theft. Even the knowledge of it is a theft . . . of sorts.

The blue is the Ideal. It is not only exclusive but practically unattainable. It is the "original" in that it is an intangible, unknowable form, in the Platonic sense. The grey is the common experience or phenomenon. What is of interest here in the artifice of the cardboard painted blue, for like a word or a play it stands mid-way between an action and the idea of that, taking its identity from both but identical to neither. The artifice is just that; it is an artifice. It is a conscious creation. It is, however, as a result of the hands of the craftsman, no longer grey and yet not quite identical to the object, for it is neither purely an emanation, in the neo-Platonic sense, nor is it uncreate or original.

However, if both the cardboard made blue as well as the model of the replica are merely finite, imperfect imitations, one must question the very act of resorting to such forms if they, like words, must inevitably fall short of what they attempt to portray or describe. While both the discussions of the model in *Tiny Alice* and the cardboard in *Listening* present the limitations of language as a mediating instrument between the abstract and the concrete, both simultaneously present the argument for the necessity of the linguistic medium, despite its imperfect status. In both cases, the model and the artifice are the only means by which the Abstraction and its relationship to the concrete may be observed and known. Ironically, the very imperfections of language may be said to be the source of its attraction for Albee since its failure to capture completely the Abstract, as it is termed in *Tiny Alice*, is what renders the Abstract comprehensible to the human intellect. Language, as the "glorious imperfect," allows the imperfect to know glory if not perfection.

As the meeting ground of the abstract and the concrete, language serves to help man understand the nature of each. Without that help, man is placed in the dilemma, so common in the plays of Albee, of not being able to distinguish between illusion and reality. This problem of illusion and reality is the exact source of Julian's dilemma in *Tiny Alice*. Such confusion is seen in Julian's remarkable description of a hallucinatory sexual encounter. Significantly, Miss Alice responds to Julian's account of his sexual/ecstatic experience with a fellow inmate by asking, "Is the memory of something having happened the same as it having happened?" Her question as to the actual relationship between the real and the imaginary remains the problem with which Julian must grapple throughout the rest of the play, and, in fact, it is central to incidents in the lives of the characters in several other plays as well, for the hallucinatory nature of sexual union is a recurring theme in the works of Albee. The theme is made manifest in *The Zoo Story* in Jerry's description of his relationship with is landlady:

> And somewhere, somewhere in the back of that pea-sized brain of hers, an organ developed just enough to let her eat, drink, and emit, she has some foul parody of sexual desire. And I, Peter, am the object of her sweaty lust.
>
> But I have found a way to keep her off. When she talks to me, when she presses herself to my body and mumbles about her

room and how I should come there, I merely say: but, Love;
wasn't yesterday enough for you, and the day before? Then she
puzzles, she makes slits of her tiny eyes, she sways a little, and
then, Peter . . . and it is at this moment that I think I might be
doing some good in that tormented house . . . a simple-minded
smile begins to form on her unthinkable face, and she giggles and
groans as she thinks about yesterday and the day before; as she
believes and relives what never happened.

For the landlady, one may indeed say that memory is the equivalent of event.
Jerry's obvious distaste over the incident shows that he, like Julian, is as
deeply affected by another's fantasy as if the actual events had taken place.
The same problem arises in *Virginia Woolf* where it is not the sexual act that
is fantasized but rather the product of that act, the imaginary son. In all of
these cases, the best evidence points to the unreality of the events described,
and yet in each case, the hallucination of the action produces the same effects
as the actual event. Hallucination, then, provides a middle ground between
idea and event for those who find the Ideal unattainable and the present
unbearable. In *Virginia Woolf*, George makes a similar observation when he
notes,

> It's very simple. . . . When people can't abide things as they are,
> when they can't abide the present, they do one of two things . . .
> either they . . . either they turn to a contemplation of the past,
> as I have done, or they set about to . . . alter the future.

Julian confirms the value of such mediation when he concludes his description
of his hallucinatory encounter by noting,

> I was persuaded, eventually, that perhaps I was . . . over-con-
> cerned by hallucination; that some was inevitable, and a portion
> of that—even desirable.

In all three instances, Albee relies on the sexual metaphor for this commin-
gling of illusion and reality, a metaphor commonly found in the writings of
the mystics in their attempts to describe mystical union. Julian's confusion,
here as well as throughout his life, is the direct result of his rejection of a
middle ground, of the possible union of the Absolute and the relative which
is achieved in both the made-over cardboard and the model of the replica.
In the third act of the play, the other characters attempt to apprise him of
this very folly:

LAWYER: *(Sarcasm is gone; all is gone, save fact.)* Dear Julian; we all serve, do we not? Each of us his own priesthood; publicly, some, others . . . within only; but we all do—what's-his-name's special trumpet, or clear lonely bell. Predestination, fate, the will of God, accident. . . . All swirled up in it, no matter what the name. And being man, we have invented choice, and have, indeed, gone further, and have catalogued the underpinnings of choice. But we do not know. Anything. End prologue.

MISS ALICE: Tell him.

LAWYER: No Matter. We are leaving you now, Julian; agents, every one of us—going. We are leaving you . . . to your accomplishment: your marriage, your wife, your . . . special priesthood.

JULIAN: *(Apprehension and great suspicion.)* I . . . don't know what you're talking about.

LAWYER: *(Unperturbed.)* What is so amazing is the . . . coming together . . . of disparates . . . left-fielding, out of the most unlikely. Who would have thought, Julian? Who would have thought? You have brought us to the end of our service here. We go on; you stay.

BUTLER: May I begin to cover?

MISS ALICE: Not Yet. *(Kindly)* Do you understand, Julian?

JULIAN: *(Barely in control.)* Of course not!

MISS ALICE: Julian, I have tried to be . . . *her.* No; I have tried to be . . . what I thought she might, what might make you happy, what you might use, as a . . . what?

BUTLER: *Play* God; go on.

MISS ALICE: We must . . . represent, draw pictures, reduce or enlarge to . . . to what we can understand.

JULIAN: *(Sad, mild.)* But I have fought against it . . . all my life. When they said, "Bring the wonders down to me, closer; I cannot see them, touch; nor can I believe." I have fought against it . . . all my life.

BUTLER: *(To Miss Alice; softly.)* You see? No good.

MISS ALICE: *(Shrugs.)* I have done what I can do with it.

JULIAN: All my life. In and out of . . . confinement, fought against the symbol.

MISS ALICE: Then you should be happy now.

CARDINAL: Julian, it has been our desire always to serve; your sense of mission.

LAWYER: We are surrogates; *our* task is done now.

MISS ALICE: Stay with her.

JULIAN: *(Horror behind it; disbelieving.)* Stay . . . with . . . her?

MISS ALICE: Stay with her. Accept it.

LAWYER: *(At the model.)* Her rooms are lighted. It is warm, there is enough.

MISS ALICE: Be content with it. Stay with her.

JULIAN: *(Refusing to accept what he is hearing.)* Miss Alice . . . I have married *you*.

MISS ALICE: *(Kind, still.)* No, Julian; you have married *her* . . . through me.

JULIAN: *(Pointing to the model.)* There is nothing there! We are *here!* There is no one *there!*

LAWYER: *She* is there . . . we believe.

JULIAN: *(To Miss Alice.)* I have been with *you!*

MISS ALICE: *(Not explaining; sort of dreamy.)* You have felt her warmth through me, touched her lips through my lips, held her hands, through mine, my breasts, hers, lain on her bed, through mine, wrapped yourself in her wings, your hands on the small of her back, your mouth on her hair, the voice in your ear, hers not mine, all hers; her. You are hers.

CARDINAL: Accept.

BUTLER: Accept.

LAWYER: Accept.

This dialogue presents the beginning of Julian's awe-filled recognition of the price exacted by his rejection of symbols, for Alice herself admits that she is merely a symbol, an imperfect attempt to present the abstract. Everyone is, as the lawyer notes, an "agent," a representative of a thing, rather than the thing itself. The wedding itself is a symbol of mediation or union. Julian as a *lay brother* is himself an apt symbol of the very kind of mediation which he has spent his life trying to reject. Yet Julian's rejection of such mediation has been his distinguishing characteristic throughout the play. The true extent of Julian's dualistic vision, as well as its dire consequences, is seen in his own account of the cause of his madness:

JULIAN: Oh . . . *(Pause.)* I . . . I lost my faith. *(Pause.)* In God.

BUTLER: Ah. *(Then a questioning look.)*

JULIAN: Is there more?

BUTLER: *Is* there more?

JULIAN: Well, nothing . . . of matter. I . . . declined. I . . .

shriveled into myself; a glass dome . . . descended, and it
seemed I was out of reach, unreachable, finally
unreaching, in this . . . paralysis, of sorts. I . . . put
myself in a mental home.

BUTLER: *(Curiously noncommittal.)* Ah.

JULIAN: I coulld not reconcile myself to the chasm between the
nature of God and the use to which man put . . . God.

BUTLER: Between your God and others', your view and theirs.

JULIAN: I said what I intended: *(Weighs the opposites in each hand.)*
It is God the mover, not God the puppet; God the
creator, not the God created by man.

BUTLER: *(Almost pitying.)* Six years in the loony bin of
semantics?

JULIAN: *(Slightly flustered, heat.)* It is not semantics! Men create a
false God in their own image, it is easier for them! . . . It
is not.

The passage is the key to Julian's thinking as it clearly shows that to Julian
the difference between the First Cause and its emanations, between an object
and the perception of that object, is both real and irreconcilable. Furthermore, the movement is essentially neo-Platonic since the contrasting movement from experience to abstraction, namely man's creation of God, is
rejected out of hand. Because the distinction is real, it is not in Julian's eyes
"semantic," that is, without substance. Julian then is rejecting what he believes to be the relative in favor of the Absolute.

In order to understand more fully the exact nature of Julian's rejection
of the label "semantic" to describe the difference between idea and emanation,
it is necessary to consider a case in which he feels that the term is appropriate:

BUTLER: *(To Julian, pointing first to the model, then to the room.)*
Do you mean the model . . . or the replica?

JULIAN: I mean the . . . I mean . . . what we are in.

BUTLER: *Ah*-ha. And which is that?

JULIAN: That we are in?

BUTLER: Yes.

LAWYER: *(To Julian.)* You are clearly not a Jesuit. *(Turning.)*
Butler, you've put him in a clumsy trap.

BUTLER: *(Shrugging.)* I'm only a servant.

LAWYER: *(To Julian, too sweetly.)* You needn't accept his
alternative . . . that since we are clearly not in a model we
must be in a replica.

BUTLER: *(Vaguely annoyed.)* Why must he not accept that?

MISS ALICE: Yes, Why not?

LAWYER: I said he did not *need* to accept the alternative. I did not say it was not valid.

JULIAN: *(Cheerfully.)* I will not accept it; the problem is only semantic.

To Julian the relationship between the model and the replica, as opposed to the relationship between God and the world, is semantic. The difference between idea and event is absolute; the differences between the various emanations of that idea are not. Language is, to Julian, part of the phenomenal. It is not, like the grey cardboard painted blue, a bridge from one realm to the other, for Julian would reject the artifice of the cardboard as an Aristotelian movement from the concrete to the abstract, since that is the movement which Julian wishes to avoid. Julian's reaction is to resolve the tension of that duality not by transcendence of the oppositions or by accepting their existence and arranging them hierarchically but rather through a complete dismissal of the phenomenal. Because Julian sees the use of symbols of a lessening of the Abstract, he rejects it out of hand. The Lawyer replies,

> I have learned . . . Brother Julian . . . never to confuse the representative of a . . . thing with the thing itself.

In other words, the corruption of the Cardinal who is the subject of the dialogue in no way diminishes the God for which he stands. The manipulation of the symbol does not affect the idea which it represents. Again, that is why the fire, although first seen in the model, must be extinguished in the replica. The destruction of the chapel must be reflected in the model for its purpose is to reflect the replica as it is, not as it was. The fire, of course, has no effect on the original which exits only in memory and is no longer affected by events in the real world. Thus, Julian's fear that symbols constitute a lessening of the Abstract is proven to be groundless.

The lawyer, with the butler acting out the role of Julian, demonstrates the folly of the confusion under which Julian suffers:

LAWYER: But *shall* we tell him the whole thing? The Cardinal? What is happening?

BUTLER: How much can he take?

LAWYER: He is a man of God, however much he simplifies, however much he worships the symbol and not the substance.

BUTLER: Like everyone.

LAWYER: Like most.

BUTLER: Julian can't stand that; he told me so: men make God in their own image, he said. Those six years I told you about.

LAWYER: Yes. When he went into an asylum. YES.

BUTLER: It was—because he could not stand it, wasn't it? The use men put God to.

LAWYER: It's perfect; wonderful.

BUTLER: Could not reconcile.

LAWYER: No.

BUTLER: God as older brother, scout leader, couldn't take that.

LAWYER: And still not reconciled.

BUTLER: Has pardoned men, I think. Is walking on the edge of an abyss, but is balancing. Can be pushed . . . over, back to the asylums.

LAWYER: Or over . . . to the Truth. *(Addressing Julian, as if he were there; some thunder in the voice.)* God, Julian? Yes? God? *Whose* God? Have you pardoned men their blasphemy, Julian? Have you forgiven them?

BUTLER: *(Quiet echoing answers; being Julian.)* No, I have not, have not really; have *let* them, but cannot accept.

LAWYER: Have not forgiven. No Julian. Could you ever?

BUTLER: *(Ibid.)* It is their comfort, my agony.

LAWYER: Soft God? The Servant? Gingerbread God with the raisin eyes?

BUTLER: *(Ibid.)* I cannot accept it.

LAWYER: Then don't accept it, Julian.

BUTLER: But there is *some*thing. There is a *true* God.

LAWYER: There is an abstraction, Julian, but it cannot be understood. You cannot worship it.

BUTLER: *(Ibid.)* There is more.

LAWYER: There is Alice, Julian. That can be understood. Only the mouse in the model. Just that.

BUTLER: *(Ibid.)* There must be more.

LAWYER: The mouse. Believe it. Don't personify this abstraction, Julian, limit it, demean it. Only the mouse, the toy. And that does not exist . . . but is all that can be worshipped. . . . Cut off from it, Julian, ease yourself, ease off. No trouble now; accept it.

BUTLER: *(Talking to Julian now.)* Accept it, Julian; ease off. Worship it.

LAWYER: Accept it.

This play within a play not only makes its point in and about the abstract but goes on to provide its corroboration in fact since the butler, named Butler in another convenient merging of idea and actuality, by acting the role of Julian has not affected Julian in any real sense. The problem, as the Lawyer sets it forth, is that the Abstract is, as Julian claims, unknowable and ineffable. Julian is correct to that extent, and yet like everyone else Julian has continued to pursue that unattainable knowledge. What sets Julian apart is his refusal to accept the necessary compromise or mediation which such a paradox demands. By refusing to accept mediation which others accept, Julian has only placed the Abstract farther beyond his reach. By rejecting symbols, Julian is abandoning all that may be known of the Absolute on the non-mystical, conscious level. Julian has ultimately deceived himself into believing that he has, in fact, completely rejected the mediation of language and symbol in his striving to experience the divine. Yet to speak and think of the Absolute as Julian does or, for that matter, even to resort to the term "Absolute" is indeed a denial of the recognition of its ineffability.

It is the recognition of this self-deception which comprises the bulk of Julian's final soliloquy. Deserted and dying at the play's conclusion, Julian realizes that in marrying Miss Alice he has, as the lawyer said, unknowingly accepted the symbol as a reality, for without the symbol "THE ABSTRACTION" is too terrible to behold. Julian's final words, as if in answer to the earlier pleas of both the lawyer and the butler are, "I accept thee, Alice, for thou art come to me. God, Alice . . . I accept thy will." The ultimate proclamation of Julian's folly, however, comes in Julian's realization that he is facing death. Julian has imagined Death, not dying. He knows life, the phenomenal, and has imagined Death, the ontological, but he has never given any thought to dying, the act of translation, the middle ground between the two.

Significantly, in the act of dying Julian assumes the attitude of the crucified Christ, another mediator between the Abstract and the concrete. Death is the ineffable state. Dying, however, may be known and described. In the last analysis, Julian is of a kind with Albee's many other characters such as Peter and Nick who are lost in the midst of verbal exchanges of which they had no understanding. However, while Julian's dilemma is ultimately linguistic in nature, he is not merely a man who cannot understand the language in which the oblique discussions of the mysterious Alice are couched. He is, until the final lines of the play, a man who will not understand because he rejects language and symbol as an unnecessary, even unacceptable compromise. He is not able to live comfortably in a world where all Truth and, therefore, meaning are in George's words, "relative." Yet, it is the very compromise which has been at the thematic and structural centers of Albee's work from its inception, and it is the basis for the playwright's initial reaction to the interviewers' question concerning the place of realism in theatre. As he has noted in several interviews, the ultimate task of the playwright is "to turn fact into truth," and this is the compromise of both the playwright and the linguist.

LIAM O. PURDON

The Limits of Reason:
Seascape *as Psychic Metaphor*

One of the most notable aspects of Edward Albee's drama has been his recurrent interest in theatre as a means for the revelation of psychological process, for by his own admission Albee has, as a writer, been most interested in capturing the unconscious rhythms of his onstage characters rather than their superficial mannerisms. Clearly, with their extensive speeches directed to multiple audiences and their diminished physical action, many of Albee's plays have as their focus the motivation behind action rather than action itself. Thus one finds that with increasing regularity Albee's work seems to include both discussions of and metaphors for the cognitive process, so that within his works virtually no explanation for human consciousness—ranging from the brief discussion of the physio-electrical basis of knowledge in *Listening* to the use of the phrenological model as a prop in the psychological allegory, *Tiny Alice*—is left unexplored. However, it is in *Seascape* that Albee provides one of his clearest attempts to render his own understanding of the human psyche into extended and concrete metaphorical form. While *Tiny Alice*, dubbed by its critics as "metafuzzical," works as an abstract treatise on human psychology, *Seascape* functions in the tradition of the medieval morality play with its more clearly defined figures serving as emblems for the distinct parts of the human consciousness.

In rendering his own version of human psychological makeup, Albee clearly borrows from but does not conspicuously adhere to the traditional psychic zones of Freudian tripartation, for the playwright does metaphori-

From *Edward Albee: An Interview and Essays*, edited by Julian N. Wasserman. © 1983 by the University of St. Thomas. The University of St. Thomas Press, 1983.

Moreover, Nancy's reference to Proust is especially significant here since, within the context of the passage, it introduces the Proustian concept of absence, one of the most revealing of the nineteenth century literary representations of the primordial life principle of the Freudian "impulsion to obtain satisfaction." This view of love as a "subjective creation of imagination which cannot thrive in the presence of its object" explains the essential motivation behind her ephemeral infidelity.

Albee completes the development of the metaphoric representation of the pleasure principle in the character of Nancy by illustrating telling idiosyncrasies of her behavior and qualifying the nature of her relationship with Charlie. Nancy, for example, is conspicuously and frequently ebullient, especially as she returns to her painting and tries to persuade Charlie "to unfetter" himself and "see everything twice." While originating in a natural desire, this ebullience, owing to its frequency, illustratees the frenetic condition of the "impulsion to satisfaction." Further, her thinking—often muddled and, as she herself points out, contradictory—degenerates frequently into emotionalism, which further illustrates the disorganized condition of desire. Likewise, her repeated demonstrations of peevishness—to which she, again, admits guilt as she states to Charlie almost perfunctorily, "I was being petulant"—reveal a disunified will. And her subordinate relationship to Charlie, which she acknowledges several times, also contributes to the metaphor of the pleasure principle in that it intimates the dynamics of mental process. This subservient status takes on significant meaning and even explains much of Nancy's argument when she begins to tell Charlie how she nearly became unfaithful and states, "The deeper your inertia went, the more *I* felt alive." As reason loses control of desire, the impulsion to satisfaction assumes a stronger vitality. Hence, Charlie's direct response shortly thereafter to Nancy's taunting—"You're not cruel by nature; it's not your way."—functions in a severalfold manner: it enables Charlie to gain the advantage in the argument, provides a statement of her character, and introduces for the audience, on the one hand, an illustration of the dynamic process by which one force keeps the other in check, and, on the other, a significant nonjudgmental account of the nature of unrestrained fulfillment of satisfaction. The primordial life function is neither good nor bad; it is just the manifestation of tremendous vitality. As Freud points out: "Naturally, the id knows no values, no good and evil, no morality."

As Albee uses the character of Nancy to illustrate the pleasure principle, so he likewise uses Charlie to embody the corresponding reality principle and its role of restraining, or counter-balancing, the uncontrolled impulses of the former. Thus, while Nancy refers to Proust, Charlie is through his own allusion associated with Anatole France, a figure noted for his rationalistic, dispassionate approach to art. While Nancy consistently reacts through the display of emotion, Charlie reacts through reason. Thus, Charlie's first reaction to the sight of Leslie and Sarah is to posit the "logical" explanation that he and Nancy have become victims of food poisoning, a logical if incorrect means of making the unknown and irrational fit neatly into the constructs of his own world. Thus, in Charlie one finds a man who finds it easier to yield up his own life, through the assumption of his own death, than to accept that which defies his own logic and experience. While Charlie first becomes distraught at the sight of the two reptilian creatures, he quickly gains control over his emotions, in contrast to Nancy, who is immediately attracted to the creatures precisely because they seem so alien and, hence, apart from ordinary, rational experience.

However, if Charlie and Nancy are so different in their initial responses to life in general and the sea-creatures in particular, it would be a mistake to conceive of their midlife crisis as being analogous to that of the anonymous pair in *Counting the Ways*, whose lives are shown to have grown so separate and self-contained, for the point of conflict between Nancy and Charlie is the way in which their differently directed points of view act upon each other in order to create a workable psychological balance which allows them to function successfully in the world at large. Thus, Charlie and Nancy cannot ultimately be examined in isolation since both of their identities come from the continual tug-of-war between their conflicting desires, a conflict which results in their perpetual process of dynamic self-definition and their mutual dependency rather than separateness. One sees this self-defining tug-of-war in Nancy's attempt to convince Charlie to relive his boyhood experience of submerging himself in the ocean. Charlie points out to Nancy that as a child he enjoyed sensory delight and the condition of being submerged and contained in the water:

> I used to go way down; at our summer place; a protective cove. The breakers would come in with a storm, or a high wind, but not usually. I used to go way down, and try to stay. I remember before that, when I was tiny, I would go to the swimming pool, at the shallow end, let out my breath and sit on the bottom . . . and when I was older, we were by the sea. Twelve; yes, or thirteen.
>
> I used to lie on the warm boulders, strip off . . . learn about my body . . . And I would go into the water, take two stones, as large as I could manage, swim out a bit, tread, look up one

final time at the sky . . . relax . . . begin to go down . . . just
one more object come to the bottom, or living thing, part of the
undulation and silence. It was very good.

Clearly, Charlie's description of this world of "undulation and silence"
is one of a state of pre-consciousness, of the mind free and unrestricted by
reason and, especially, social convention which restrains impulse. Nancy's
prolonged insistence that Charlie attempt to re-enact what has become just
a pleasant and remote memory is her attempt to convert Charlie into her
own image by returning him to a type of prelapsarian state of consciousness.
Significantly, Charlie's stern resistance to this letting go of the conscious
world is rooted in his self-consciousness, his awareness of himself as an adult.
As in the case of Nancy's early sexual urges, it is the category, or role,
imposed from without which ultimately separates Charlie from the pleasures
of his youth. For both Charlie and Nancy, then, the result of this verbal
give and take concerning desire and restraint is a process of self-definition
through assertion and defense of their own points of view as each tries to
defend his own values while converting those of the other.

Having established the tenuous balance between the two parts of the
waking consciousness, Albee proceeds to examine and test that balance
through the introduction of the two saurian creatures who have as their
origin the hidden, subconscious world of "undulation and silence" described
by Charlie, much as the playwright does with Jerry's entrance into the well
ordered, conventional world of Peter in *The Zoo Story* as well as in the
unexpected appearance of Elizabeth in *The Lady from Dubuque*. If the appearance of the saurian creatures is intended as a litmus test of the central
characters, the differences between Charlie and Nancy become apparent
almost immediately. However, in order to understand these differences, it
is important to recognize an important but subtle metamorphosis which
occurs within the play. The first part of the play, the initial debate between
Charlie and Nancy takes place in the realm of ordinary consciousness, the
world of reason. It is a world in which Charlie, as a symbol of reason and
convention, acts as indolent restraint on the more active pleasure principle.
The interjection of reason into that world is symbolized by the intrusive
sounds of jet aircraft into the naturalistic scenery of the first act. The jets,
whose sounds are heard some four times within the first act, are represen-
tatives, *par excellence*, of controlling rationality—for they are non-natural
machines created through reason in order to satisfy and, hence, channel the
primordial, imaginative urge to fly.

With the appearance of Leslie and Sarah that world is transformed into a realm in which the laws no longer apply and where the non-rational is in control. In this made-over world, the jet airplanes, whose presence were so strongly and frequently felt in the first act, make only one brief appearance. The terror which they inspire in Leslie and Sarah as well as the discomfort they create for Nancy show just how alien such machines are to nature. Within this context even the "reasonable" Charlie doubts their worth— "They'll crash into the dunes one day; I don't know what good they do"— with the result that he repeatedly emphasizes their status as mere "machines" whose imitation of the flight of birds is as unsatisfactory and incomplete as he had earlier judged a parrot's unthinking mimicry of human speech to be. Thus the formerly lethargic Charlie becomes active and aggressive and has to be restrained by the previously restive Nancy. From the first appearance of the saurian creatures, Nancy has clearly been in control. She is the first to notice their approach. As she recalls her childhood desires, she sees Leslie and Sarah emerge from the water; as she and Charlie discuss the possibility of Charlie's submerging himself, she notices that the two visitors are lying prone on the beach; and as she almost cajoles Charlie into slipping into the water, she observes that she has lost track of Leslie and Sarah. Nancy is also the first to recognize the intrinsic beauty of the visitors, although, in keeping with the function of her characterization, she does not know why she finds them aesthetically pleasing. Thus, as Charlie recoils at the sight of Leslie and Sarah and assumes a defensive posture, Nancy almost dreamily responds to Charlie's commands, extolling Leslie's and Sarah's beauty, first, with "Charlie! They're magnificent!" and, later, with "Charlie, I think they're absolutely beautiful. What are they?"

Yet if Nancy is in her element, Charlie clearly is not. From the outset, the reason and restraint which he demonstrated in the first part of the play repeatedly fail him in his dealings with the saurian intruders. His rational explanation for the appearance of the creatures as a result of "bad liver paste" is painfully inadequate, even to the non-rational, intuitive Nancy. And with the movement into the non-rational world, the playwright's function becomes the demonstration of the failure of rationality in the face of the irrational. This is, of course, a familiar theme in many of Albee's works, such as *A Delicate Balance* and *Tiny Alice*, and is no doubt responsible for Albee's interest in and adaptation of Herman Melville's "Bartleby the Scrivener." Thus, as reason breaks down, Albee proceeds to give the unconscious a conscious form just as, when the restraints of marriage weakened, Nancy found herself giving form to her fantasies of premarital encounters with young men. Yet what is unique about *Seascape* is that, while Leslie's and Sarah's appearance suggests promordiality, it is not their saurian physical natures but rather the lengthy and seemingly desultory conversations which they have with Charlie and Nancy that confirm their introduction as representations of psychic energy. On the one hand, these discussions reveal an absence of the laws of logic; on the other, they demonstrate a disregard for or ignorance of social convention, moral restraint, and cognitive awareness of the totality of being—in other words, the artificial restraints imposed from without upon the "impulsion to satisfaction." In this regard, Leslie and Sarah also provide a view of the source of aggression and desire, another principal aspect of libido.

As the two couples encounter each other at the beginning of act 2, they reveal fear and a lack of trust. No sooner do they introduce themselves to each other than they begin a series of dialogues which, while intended to be informative, end in futility, without the exchange of any meaningful information. Significantly, the first of these dialogues concerns eating. Interestingly, it also introduces the correlative condition of the ignorance of social convention. Charlie points out to Leslie that he does not know Leslie's eating habits. He then adds that "It'd be perfectly normal to assume you [that is, Leslie and Sarah] ate whatever . . . you ran into . . . you know, whatever you ran into." Leslie's ingenious response—"No; I don't know"—reveals the weakness of Charlie's assumption. But the absurdity of the assumption is not exposed until Charlie, who is striving for a simple response to Leslie's initial inquiry regarding Nancy's and his disposition, states that he and Nancy do not eat "anything that talks; you know, English." Nancy at this turn in the dialogue points out that parrots do talk and that people eat parrots. This revelation not only emphasizes the illogic of Charlie's second generalization, which is reinforced by Leslie who asks, "What are you saying?" but also brings the dialogue to an abrupt halt, as Charlie attempts a restatement of his original assumption, saying "I'm trying to tell you . . . we don't eat our own kind." Charlie does not contradict himself, but his attempt to sustain his original assumption undermines itself and meaning vanishes.

Another exchange that brings to the fore the absence of logic appears shortly afterward as Nancy shows Sarah her breasts. As in the first case, this instance also provides another view of the ignorance of social convention on the parts of the saurian creatures. The passage in question begins with the discussion of the function of clothing, another artificial convention, but soon focuses on the subject of Nancy's breasts. While Nancy conducts herself in a straightforward manner and shows no shame in the hope of enlightening Leslie and Sarah who have never seen a mammalian breast, Charlie becomes irrational at the seeming breakdown of decorum. At first Charlie demonstrates a postlapsarian prudishness when he corrects Nancy, indicating that she should say "mammary" instead of "breast." Next, when Sarah ingenuously beckons Leslie to see Nancy's breasts, Charlie reveals possessiveness, stating that he does not want Leslie looking at Nancy's nakedness. But when Charlie is questioned by Nancy and Leslie as to the motivation for his possessiveness and Leslie states conditionally that he does not want to see Nancy's breasts, Charlie reverses his original attitude, defending and extolling the virtue and beauty of Nancy's anatomy: "They're not embarrassing; *or* sad! They're lovely! Some women . . . some women . . . Nancy's age, they're . . . some women . . . I *love* your breasts." While Charlie's about-face can certainly be viewed as a positive act of acceptance, it reveals the working of the emotional rather than the cognitive consciousness because it is predicated upon pride and follows a demonstration of repressive social behavior. It is no coincidence, then, that Albee includes in his stage directions for Charlie that he is "more flustered than angry." What Charlie achieves is what he needs to achieve; that he finally perceives beauty through the challenging of his possessive nature, however, demonstrates the absence of logic.

While several other instances of emotionalism and non sequiturs appear in this act, the discussion of ontology provides the best example of the suspension of the laws of reason. In an effort to explain why they are dead, the absurdity of which cannot go unnoticed, Charlie tries to explain to Leslie that created reality is an illusion and that true existence comes about through thought. Instead of being logical, Charlie becomes flustered and angry, and the dialogue degenerates into an emotional bout which concludes ironically with Charlie's losing control of himself, shouting the name of Descartes:

LESLIE: Then I take it *we* don't *exist*.

CHARLIE: *(Apologetic.)* Probably not; I'm sorry.

LESLIE: *(To Nancy.)* That's quite a mind he's got there.

NANCY: *(Grudgingly defending Charlie.)* Well . . . he thinks things through. (Very cheerful.) As for *me*, I couldn't care less; I'm having far too interesting a time.

SARAH: *(Gets on all fours.)* Oh, I'm so glad!

LESLIE: *(Comes three steps down L. ridge. Puzzled.)* I *think* I exist.

CHARLIE: *(Shrugs.)* Well, that's all that matters; it's the same thing.

CHARLIE: What?

LESLIE: What you *said*.

CHARLIE: *(Barely in control.)* DESCARTES!! DESCARTES!! I THINK: THEREFORE I AM!! *(Pause.)* COGITO ERGO SUM! I THINK: THEREFORE I AM.

Leslie's comment that Charlie has "quite a mind" adds a further touch of irony, but it is Charlie's final comment concerning death as a release that confirms that logic has indeed failed. That Charlie beckons death by describing the final moments of life shows that he prefers the dissolution of life or existence and, in turn, the absence of reason. While the sound of an airplane flying overhead ends the discussion, the actual termination of the exchange of ideas, then, occurs in Charlie's demonstration of emotion. Even with the invocation of Descartes, the laws of logic remain absent.

The final fight or disagreement which draws the play to a close might also be viewed as another instance of the suspension of the laws of logic. Charlie's attempt to make Sarah cry is certainly irrational; this persistent taunting is clearly cruel. But the fight also introduces another view of the unconscious; it reveals an account of aggression. As Charlie forces Sarah to admit that she would cry her heart out if Leslie ever left her, Leslie grabs Charlie by the throat and slowly strangles him. Leslie's act of aggression is a demonstration of brute force, but as Leslie himself implies shortly afterward in the line "Don't you talk to me about brute beast," Charlie's remorseless questioning illustrates a verbal manifestation of the same act. Leslie's implication also clarifies Charlie's previous statements concerning Leslie and Sarah. When Charlie begins the confrontation which nearly leads to his own strangulation, he exclaims that he does not understand his own feelings toward Leslie and Sarah: "I don't *know* what more I want. *(To Leslie and Sarah.)* I don't know what I want for *you.* I don't know what I feel toward you; it's either love or loathing. Take your pick." While Charlie's ambivalence represents a lack of conscious control, the fact that he does describe his feelings toward Leslie and Sarah as being either of love or loathing represents an acknowledgment of Leslie and Sarah as being either the source of aggression or of desire.

Several other minor instances of aggression also arise in the second act, such as Charlie's continued taunting of Leslie and Sarah, but the one that brings the question of the unconscious clearly to the fore, like the fight in the conclusion, occurs when Charlie questions Sarah's fidelity. Charlie gets Sarah to admit that she has not "coupled" with anyone but Leslie; however, Leslie, who, like Nancy, is confused by the line of questioning, asks Charlie to state precisely what "are you after." When Charlie cannot and evades making an attempt at a conceptual understanding of his own purpose, a fight nearly breaks out—Nancy's and Sarah's joint intercession notwithstanding. The conflict which arises, then, results partly from Charlie's effrontery but mostly from a breakdown in communication. Ironically, it is Charlie, not Leslie, who is incapable of maintaining symbolic logic, although he blames Leslie for his own ineffectuality when he condescendingly adds, "Especially to someone who has no grasp of conceptual matters, who hasn't heard of half the words in the English language, who lives on the bottom of the sea and has green scales!"

This representation of aggression resulting from the absence of conceptual ability introduces a third way in which Albee creates the metaphor of uncontrolled psychic energy. Throughout the second act, he calls attention to the need for and the absence of a cognitive awareness of the totality of being. The latter obviously appears in all of the instances of aggression and lack of logic that appear from the moment the second act begins. The former, on the other hand, appears twice: first, early in the act, as Charlie and Leslie enter into a discussion of anatomical differences and, second, as Nancy and Charlie later attempt to explain and define the concept of emotion for Leslie and Sarah. In the discussion of the anatomical differences, Leslie and Sarah learn the distinctions between toes and fingers, arms and legs. This knowledge then leads them to an understanding of the social convention of handshaking, which they perform enthusiastically. While the information allows Leslie and Sarah to experience something they have never known, the significance of the event lies in the fact that it represents the beginning of the fusion of the conscious, embodied by Nancy and Charlie, and the unconscious self, embodied by Leslie and Sarah. In the later discussions of emotion, the same thing happens but to a greater degree. As Nancy and Charlie explain the nature of emotion to Leslie and Sarah, not only do the two couples gradually overcome the differences that separate them, but each couple also gains its own emotional equilibrium. Charlie and Nancy work out the doubts that each has felt toward the other; Leslie and Sarah learn what love is. Furthermore, through the delineation of emotion and the attainment of the awareness of social convention, Nancy and Charlie discover the means by which to keep Leslie and Sarah from retreating to the sea. Thus, as Albee indicates in the conclusion, it is through the understanding of the physical that one begins to perceive the totality of his being, but it is through the examination of the emotions, difficult as it may be, that one attains the totality of being.

Seascape, then, is much more than a fantastic dramatic experience. Like many of Albee's other plays, it is a romance. It provides a view of order in the presentation of the metaphoric representations of the reality and pleasure principles and a dissolution of that order in the symbolic representation of psychic energy. Like all romances, it possesses an essentially comic structure and so offers a resolution to the dissolution. Symbolically, that resolution appears in the form of a handshake. But as the conclusion to the second act demonstrates, the means by which order is reestablished is through the maintaining of contact with and the understanding of the subconscious: hence, the function of Nancy's unremitting insistence in the closing moments of the play that Leslie and Sarah not leave. To attain consciousness, as Albee indicates, one must be willing to enter the seascape, or Charlie's "protected cove," where land and sea—consciousness and the unconscious—meet and learn to accept the meaning of the experience. In that sense, *Seascape*, with its face-to-face confrontation between its creatures of the land and the sea, is not the flawed tale of unanswered evolutionary questions often described by critics but is, instead, an optimistic blueprint for the development of a higher consciousness, for in Albee's mind evolution is clearly a matter of consciousness rather than form.

THOMAS P. ADLER

The Pirandello in Albee:
The Lady from Dubuque

"Reality is too little for me."
—Listening

I'll make toast; I'll make buttered toast.
That will be heaven. Won't that be
heaven, Oscar?
Well, it will be toast.
—The Lady from Dubuque

Although Edward Albee's *The Lady from Dubuque* was neither a critical nor a popular success when it opened on Broadway early in 1980 only to close precipitately after twelve performances, Otis Guernsey, Jr. rightly includes it among *The Best Plays of 1979–1980*, predicting with some justification, I suspect, that "this distinguished and durable play . . . will surely be heard in time, globally." From one point of view, *Lady from Dubuque* is a continuation of several stylistic and thematic and structural themes in Albee's plays. It is related, for example, in its corruscating wit and sometimes bitter exchanges between hosts and guests to *Who's Afraid of Virginia Woolf?* (1962); in its focus on the rights and responsibilities of family and friends to *A Delicate Balance* (1966); and in its form as a death-watch to *All Over* (1971). From yet another perspective, however, it is a culmination of Albee's interest in epistemological and ontological problems, a strand that can be traced back through *Counting the Ways* and *Listening* (1976), the pair of lengthy one-act

From *Edward Albee: An Interview and Essays*, edited by Julian N. Wasserman. © 1983 by the University of St. Thomas. The University of St. Thomas Press, 1983.

plays written immediately preceding it, and to *Tiny Alice* (1964). Even a cursory examination of *Dubuque*'s language reveals Albee's interest in—almost obsession with—the problem of knowing. The word "know" recurs, in fact, again and again in the text as both the play's characters and audience are asked to consider exactly who and what can actually be known—for within the play we are asked if we can, indeed, know ourselves or others, substances or only surfaces, essences or only their representations. Moreover, the play goes on to challenge its audience with questions concerning not only the content of our knowledge but the very process by which we come to know. *Tiny Alice* forces us to question the dependability of knowledge obtained in the most usual fashion, through the reading of observable phenomena, by asking if our merely thinking something makes it so.

The central metaphysical concern of *Tiny Alice* is clearly the problem of finite man's understandable tendency to question the reality of what cannot be perceived by the senses and, following from that, the almost universal human need to concretize the abstract, to discover or—barring that—to create a manageable representation of the unknown. Brother Julian, the play's central figure, finds upsetting and disorienting man's anthropomorphizing habit through which he simplifies mystery in order to control what cannot be understood. The widespread need to "represent" something before it can be worshipped plunges him into a dark night of the soul, for to "personify," to resort to symbolism, is to "limit it, demean it." That anthropomorphizing frame of mind is rendered visually in the stage setting: in the library of the mansion where the action occurs is a model of the mansion, exact in all its details. Perhaps, it is hinted, there is even a miniature model of this model in the library *within* the model! Ultimately, the play moves its audience toward a direct confrontation with the epistemological question of which came first: the model or the mansion? If the mansion, then the model is merely a shadow of a pre-existing form; if the model, then the mansion is only a replica of the model. A similar question can be asked of the characters on stage: are there also miniatures of them in the model? And, if so, is the onstage library simply a room within a larger model, with characters watching these characters watching?

Of those characters, Julian is a priest of the cult of "THE ABSTRACT," which for him is the only "REAL" and True. Yet, paradoxically—and herein lies the crux of his test—he can only finally achieve spiritual union with the abstract Tiny Alice (so named perhaps to suggest the very diminishment of the gods he has always rebelled against) by marrying and uniting sexually (again, a descent from the spiritual to the physical) with her surrogate, Miss Alice. So has not Julian, then, ultimately "confuse[d] the representative of a . . . thing with the thing itself? As a last, desperate defense against his fear of the Void—against the possibility that not only has he "worship[ped] the symbol and not the substance" but that no substance resides behind the symbol, that "THERE IS NOTHING THERE!"—Julian must, through a tremendous act of faith that is one of the illusions Albee claims all men use to get through life, *will* the presence of Tiny Alice at the point of his death so that his sacrifice on her altar will not have been in vain. In this most philosophically Absurd of Albee's plays, he asks: How many dimensions of multi-layered reality are real, and how many simply a figment of man's imaginings? Finally, maybe only the mouse in the model or the wig-adorned phrenological head (which diagrams man's organs of knowing) can be worshipped. But the unsettling possibility remains that those, too, have no objective existence.

Counting the Ways likewise hinges on the distinction between "knowing" as a certainty and only "thinking" that something is so as a supposition. What is at question here, though, is not metaphysical truth, but the truth of the emotions. Each desiring from the other an auricular assurance and measurement, the man and the woman (called simply "He" and "She") ask of each other, "Do you love me?" But to quantify what is essentially qualitative, to measure depth of feelings by words is, as Lear learned too late, to reduce. In *The Lady from Dubuque*, it will be the pain of dying and loss that cannot be measured, and because of its futility, such attempts at measuring the unmeasurable inevitably become little more than childish games. Within *Counting the Ways*, such Lear-like attempts to measure love inevitably result in games such as "She loves me? She loves me not?" or "Me loves he? Not me loves he?"—the latter while putting the petals back on. In the end, such games are so obviously incapable of proving that one loves or is loved that the lovers are ultimately left to live on faith in the same way that Julian dies on faith. But in this "Vaudeville," the question of knowing extends as well to the actors' and audience's awareness and perception of themselves. When a "sign descends" and lights up commanding, "IDENTIFY YOURSELVES," the actors step out of their roles as characters, address the audience now as actors (as they earlier had as characters) and improvise a thumbnail sketch of themselves, sending the audience to consult their programs "*after* the play" if they desire more information about the real lives of the actor and actress playing He and She. But to what extent can that sketch or the printed biography consisting of external facts and figures really define the person? And when the sign descends, the members of the audience might have the uneasy feeling at first that *they* are each being required to identify themselves to the others sitting arround them.

If *Tiny Alice* asks about knowing religious truth and *Counting the Ways* about ascertaining truths of the heart, *Listening* explores one's ability to know and, thus, to control the psyche of another person. In this Strindbergian "Chamber Play," The Woman, whom we take to be an analyst in a psychiatric hospital, can manipulate and ultimately drive the patient/inmate Girl to suicide. The Woman is literal-minded, cold, emotionless, rational—so calculating that her extreme rationality becomes a kind of Iago-like rationalism devoid of moral scruple or consideration. By knowing the way in which The Girl's mind works, The Woman is able to prompt The Girl to use the sharp glass in the empty fountain to slit her own wrists. Able to perceive "the movement, when an idea happens," The Woman tells The Girl, "I can hear your pupils widen." Playing on The Girl's fear of blood (menstruation) by graphically describing the analogous case history of another female patient, The Woman will drive the girl to suicide just as surely as The Woman has already driven The Man to tears by turning away from and rejecting him in a previous encounter since, as The Man points out, "Effect comes *after* act." The full force of The Woman's diabolical power of suggestion is seen in the Hedda-like line, "Done beautifully," as The Girl holds up her bleeding wrists. So The Woman has indeed been "listening" all along to the signals the psychotic Girl has been sending out.

This consistent concern on the part of the playwright with what and how people can know—or hope to know—in the metaphysical, emotional, and psychic spheres in all of these works suggests Albee's position about reality as multi-layered and essentially unknowable in any but a relativistic sense—one of the hallmarks of Pirandello's thought as well. Moreover, these brief remarks perhaps disclose other hints of Pirandello's recurrent emphases: on the fragmentation and multiplicity of personality; on the convergence and/or contrast between life and theater, role-playing and reality, the mask and its wearer; and on the audience's self-reflexivity. And in light of these themes, *The Lady from Dubuque*, which insists on the necessity to perceive life as essentially multi-leveled, seems to be Albee's most Pirandellian play to date.

Clearly, the most obviously Pirandellian aspect of *The Lady from Dubuque* is the audience's awareness that they are watching a play—an awareness pursued thematically by Pirandello in such works as *Six Characters in Search of an Author* and *Tonight We Improvise*, which are aesthetic inquiries into the nature of the theatre—extends to *The Lady from Dubuque*, wherein Albee exploits this modernist convention of making the audience conscious of themselves *as* audience by having the characters address them directly in either brief remarks or longer speeches some eighty or so times. As his "Performance Note" indicates, "this is done without self-consciousness, quite openly, and without interrupting the flow of the play." As with much of *The Lady from Dubuque*, the device does not depart from Albee's earlier practice, extending back through *Counting the Ways* (where, as we have noticed, the technique is employed adroitly and purposefully), *Box* and *Quotations from Chairman Mao Tse-Tung* (1968), *The American Dream* (1961), and even *The Sandbox* (1960). In *The American Dream*, Grandma, the most realistically conceived among characters who are deliberately drawn as cartoon figures, steps out of her role and stands back from the action to comment upon it, becoming, in a sense, a member of the audience. Similarly, *The Sandbox* is the first instance in Albee in which Pirandellian motifs—illusion/reality, play-acting, life/art—become a concern, as well as the first to employ characters as symbol, myth, and archetype.

To be sure, the self-conscious, Pirandellian lines which the characters in *The Lady from Dubuque* speak directly to the audience serve several functions. Sometimes, they simply furnish exposition; at other times, they provide the kind of editorializing to underscore a point that we ordinarily expect from a choral character. Infrequently, they are philosophic or nostalgic or sardonic meditations on some facet of existence. Often, their tone is defensive or mildly conspiratorial, demanding some complicity from the audience in the form of a supportive or empathic response in the face of a challenge issuing from one of the other characters. No matter what their purpose, however, Albee insists emphatically that in every instance these lines be spoken not by the actors as actors (as had been the case in *Counting the Ways*), but instead by the actors *in* character. As his stage directions indicate, "It is of the utmost importance that the actors make it clear that it is not they, but the characters, who are aware of the presence of the audience." Furthermore, these lines are not in the nature of "asides" as traditionally understood in drama, since the other onstage characters hear them and respond to them as they normally would to dialogue exchanges. Indeed, many of these lines are addressed simultaneously to the other characters and across the footlights to the audience. So while this technique is non-illusionistic—deliberately heightening our awareness that we are in a theatre watching a play—this device ultimately requires not so much that we reflect on ourselves as an audience but rather that we regard ourselves as, and associate ourselves with, the onstage characters who represent us. We are among the guests at this party-turned-deathwatch. Instead of being mere observers, we—though silent—are participants in this ritual. Here, then, Albee shifts emphasis from audience as audience to audience as character.

In regard to *The Lady from Dubuque*, the action which the audience is

expected both to bear witness to and take a part in might well be termed a
"coming of death" play, with Elizabeth, *The Lady from Dubuque*, and her
black companion Oscar as the summoners; yet the drama is radically different
from the medieval morality plays in theme and tone, since it reveals no
specifically religious orientation. Nor does it end with any assurance of
salvation in an afterlife. And, too, the play focuses much less on the dying
person than it does on the survivor, thus linking it closely to *All Over*. Jo,
dying of an unspecified disease which has all the symptoms of cancer, vents
her pain and bitterness on the friends who gather around, "need[ing] a surface
to bounce it all off of." Knowing that she must not succumb to self-pity,
that if she cries for herself she might fall totally apart, she requires also a
husband who possesses the necessary strength to see her through her last
agony—as she becomes less and less, as she finally joins "The very dead;
who hear nothing; who remember nothing; who are nothing." Her husband
Sam, however, also knows his needs, especially the necessity to "hold on to
the object we're losing" and not let go, as Jo diminishes "To bone? To air?
To dust?," but these needs threaten to render him impotent in responding
to Jo's. He resents, though, any intrusion from others who might try to
fulfill some of his role for him. Perhaps understandably, yet surely self-
indulgently, he needs to be the only sufferer. If Elisabeth Kübler-Ross, in
On Death and Dying, is correct in positing that the survivor must undergo
the same stages as the victim in eventually arriving at an acceptance of death,
then Sam cannot make that leap to detachment, which involves a growth
from thinking only of one's self to selflessness. Although the Lady from
Dubuque assures him, "you don't know what it *is*," Sam sobs, "I'm dying."
For in Albee's dramas, the survivors exit under a peculiar burden not felt
by the victims: not only must they live seeing the process of dying, but they
must continue on after the death and the finality which means aloneness.
They must, in short, suffer *after* the suffering has ceased for the dead. As
the widowed Long-Winded Lady in *Box* and *Quotations* notes: "But what
about *me!* . . . I . . . *am* left . . . his dying is all over; all gone, but his *death*
stays . . . *he* had only his dying. I have both."

Yet, the crux of Sam's suffering is not that he will go on alone, though
that is surely a part of it, or even that he evidently has no religious belief
to sustain him—though in any case religion is most often, in Albee, simply
one of the many illusions that man falls back on. Rather, it is Sam's inability
to plumb the mystery of "things [he] would not be expected to understand,"
to know what the moment of death will be like. He desires the certainty
that, at the point of her death, Jo have "No time to be afraid"—and by
extension that he, too, will not have time for fear either. And although

Elizabeth grants him that assurance, he can still not be absolutely certain of that fact. What is proffered in place of that certainty, or of any hope grounded in a religious system, is the fact of a multi-layered reality. Since, in Pirandello-fashion, Sam can know neither his own identity (either in games or in life) nor that of death, all he can hope to know and all he needs to know is that existence moves not just on a literal but, ritualistically, on a symbolic, metaphoric, and archetypal plane as well.

Within *The Lady from Dubuque*, Albee alludes explicitly to Pirandello's *It Is So! (If You Think So!)*. When Elizabeth remarks to Sam, "You have a woman upstairs. You *say* she is your wife; I say she is my daughter," we recall the tension between Signor Ponza and his mother-in-law Signora Frola over the identity of Signora Ponza. Ponza claims that his wife is not Signora Frola's daughter, but instead his second wife who simply pretends, for the sake of the older woman, to be her deceased daughter. Signora Frola, on the other hand, insists that Ponza has only been deluded into thinking that her daughter is his second wife in order to assuage the guilt he feels over having treated her so badly that she needed to be sent to a sanatorium. The other characters in Pirandello's play demand to know the absolute truth about Signora Ponza's identity, not really for the sake of the truth but because they are meddling busybodies intent on settling on a single, comfortable interpretation of observable phenomena, without regard for the family's suffering and vulnerability. They demand that reality not be relative, that identity be fixed and not fluid, that existence by knowable. For Pirandello, however—and herein resides the existential dilemma in his drama—truth is multiple and subjective, as he insists when he has Signora Ponza say at the close of the play that she is both Signora Frola's daughter *and* Ponza's second wife. And it is such hallmarks of Pirandellianism as the multiplicity of personality and the relativity of truth that Albee carries over into his own drama. *Dubuque's* Oscar, in the fragmentation and adaptability of his role and personality, is analogous, finally, to Signora Ponza. Even before the dying Jo mistakes him for Sam come to her aid in her last moments, Oscar has been quite willing to shift his identity to meet the demands and objections of the other characters: when Edgar, for example, refuses to believe that Oscar learned judo while serving in the Foreign Legion, Oscar replies, "Then I *wasn't* in the Foreign Legion, I don't care."

That so much of the surface action in *The Lady from Dubuque* revolves around game-playing puts us in mind of the mask/wearer dichotomy and the life/theatre and stage/world metaphors that abound in Pirandello's plays. For instance, Albee structures one of his games as a play-within-the-play in which Sam and Carol gull the other characters who are then cast as an

outraged audience to their ruse. Carol returns from the powder room, feign-
ing the violated maiden in exaggerated fashion and claiming that Sam has
attempted to seduce her. By playing this role, she manages to elicit a response
of threatened manhood from her fiancé Fred, who can see nothing but the
surface appearance which he immediately accepts as the truth. Fred's outraged reaction is only a humorous inversion and reduction of the kind of
hysteria which everyone experiences when his or her own certainty is shaken.
In his already tense condition, Sam, when faced with the unexpected appearance of Elizabeth and Oscar, is especially susceptible to anxiety over
the unknown. Verbally, Albee underscores the convergence of his concerns
with those of Pirandello by having Carol "dogmatic[ally], if uncertain[ly]"
proclaim, "Things are either true or they're not" as if reality were amenable
to a kind of either/or simplification instead of the both/and complexity which
characterizes the human predicament. When Elizabeth insists that "Everything is true," she demands the same sort of acquiescence to subjective reality
that Signora Ponza does. Yet if, for Pirandello, such assent to the multiplicity
of truth renders each person's reality as "real" as that of the next—leaving
every person with at least the assurance of his or her own subjective certainty—for Albee the suspicion always remains that if, indeed, "Everything
is true," then "nothing is true." All solipsistically perceived realities become
just another of the many illusions we depend upon to see us through life.
If, for Pirandello's characters, there still exists the possibility for attaining
individual certainty among an infinite number of relativities, for Albee's, on
the other hand, even that much certainty seems in doubt and is, perhaps,
just a desperate grasping after straws.

Thus, like several earlier Albee characters—(Harry and Edna from
Delicate Balance and Leslie and Sarah from *Seascape* (1975) among them)—our
Lady from Dubuque and her companion demand to be perceived on something other than just the literal level, as is clearly apparent from the text.
First, instead of coming in through the doors which are used by the other
characters, Elizabeth and Oscar "enter the set from one side, *from without
the set*" (emphasis added). Moreover, Elizabeth's first line "we *are* in time,"
is ambiguous in the way that many lines in the later Albee are: It may mean
that they have arrived before Jo dies, but it might just as well, especially
given Albee's own emphasis on the word "*are*," indicate that they have entered
the dimension of time from somewhere out of time. Sam's persistent question
when he comes upon them the next morning, "Who are you?"—uttered ten
times in four pages—linguistically echoes the line that the other characters
addressed to Sam at the beginning of the first act when they were playing
the game of Twenty Questions with each guest assuming an identity which

the others tried to ascertain. As though he were still playing the guessing game from the night before, Sam now asks Elizabeth if she claims to be Jo's mother. Clearly, Elizabeth does not appear to be she; Jo's mother, we are told, is "tiny, thin as a rail, blue eyes—darting furtive blue eyes . . . pale hair, tinted pink, balding a little," whereas the character description tells us Elizabeth is "a stylish, elegant, handsome woman." Furthermore, Elizabeth hails from Dubuque rather than New Jersey. A mythical creation of *New Yorker* editor Harold Ross, the Lady from Dubuque became an archetype of the kind of reader the magazine was supposedly not appealing to and refused to play down to. She is, thus, an imaginary creature who has entered into the collective imagination and who is talked about as if she really existed. Jo, it is true, does feel that her real mother has deserted her; yet if no reason exists for believing that Elizabeth is Jo's mother, there is, as one of the guests comments, just as little reason for believing that she is not. Like the endless riddle of the model and the mansion in *Tiny Alice*, The Pirandellian drama of Elizabeth's "true" identity can never be resolved and is never intended to be. Analogically, however, Elizabeth is the archetypal mother to whose care Jo returns at death. The ambiguously inflected "Dear, great God, woman" which Sam addresses to Elizabeth might be heard not as a profane expletive but rather as a reverent epithet. In the dream vision which Elizabeth recounts, she talks of seagulls, surf, and the sunset—all images for freedom and death.

Oscar, who might be seen as a kind of "angel of death" in the tradition of that character from Albee's early playlet *The Sandbox* (1959), assumes Sam's role as helpmate to Jo as she crosses the threshold from dying to death. Dressed like Sam in his distinctive sleeping gown, "arms wide, beatific," Oscar asks: "Am I not . . . am I, indeed, not Sam?" In the game at the opening of the play, Sam had pretended that he was Romulus and Remus; at the close of the play, Oscar is, in a sense, Sam's twin: morally he performs the action which Sam is incapable of undertaking. He possesses a strength which Sam lacks, carrying Jo up the stairs for the last time and easing her into death. If Elizabeth is the Lady from Dubuque and archetypal mother, Oscar is the comforting angel Sam fails to be. Since Sam cannot really be a husband to Jo in her need, that role is fulfilled by Oscar, who is his double. And just as, ironically, this Lady from Dubuque is more cognizant and knowing than the other characters, so, too, Oscar—though black—is not a demonic twin or double. If he is the Romulus who "kills" or replaces the Remus/Sam, it is only because Jo cannot wait for Sam's help.

At the very end, Sam is still asking Elizabeth, "Who are you? Really?" Of course, not knowing himself, he cannot possibly hope to know the other. The bedrock question remains the Sphinx's "Who am I" since "all of the [other] values [are] relative save" that. But then, to reach any certitude about who one is and who another is in Albee, as in Pirandello, is an impossible dream. What Sam might more profitably have done was to probe the fuller dimensions of existence by confronting the Lady from Dubuque with the question: "Who are you, metaphorically?" That, perhaps, would have been a first step in approaching the ineffable mystery at the very heart of existence—something that Carol, who began as the most bewildered of all the guests, seems able to do. She intuitively senses who and what the Lady from Dubuque and Oscar are, grasps what is happening, and honestly tries to help Sam help Jo. To see anagogically, to perceive existence as multi-leveled, is Albee's only answer to the problem of knowing that he poses in his plays. To remain always on the level of the literal reality (unknowable as even that level is) is, indeed, "too little." To know metaphorically, symbolically, archetypally is, to paraphrase Hemingway, what humankind in Albee has instead of God. Toast may be just toast, but it might also be heaven.

C. W. E. BIGSBY

Who's Afraid of Virginia Woolf?

Who's Afraid of Virginia Woolf? (1962) is set in a small New England college (the film version was shot at Smith College). Its single set, a womb-like living-room, stands as an image of a refusal of life by those who enact their fears and illusions within it. George is a professor of history married to the daughter of the college president. Unable to have children, they have conspired to create a fantasy child, designed to cement their relationship, to compensate for a delinquent reality. But in fact the child becomes a divisive principle, claimed as an accomplice by both George and Martha.

The occasion of the play is critical in terms of the myth which they have created, for the boy is on the verge of his twenty-first birthday. Thus, they are trapped by their own logic. If they sustain the myth they must let the boy go. At twenty-one his independence is an inevitable stage in his development, and a necessary concession to his supposed reality. Alternatively, if they refuse to allow him to reach his majority they will undermine a myth whose utility and whose conviction rests on the acceptance of a coincidence between real and fictional time. And witnessing this crisis is another couple, newly arrived at the university and already beginning the construction of their own illusions.

The play's three acts are entitled "Fun and Games," "Walpurgisnacht," and "The Exorcism" (the latter being the play's original title) and this progression accurately describes both Albee's method and his theme. The humour of the early part of the play gives way to a witches' sabbath in which

From *A Critical Introduction To Twentieth-Century American Drama*, volume 2. © 1984 by C. W. E. Bigsby. Cambridge University Press, 1984.

dangerous truths are exposed while the final act drives out the deadly fantasies and lays the ghost which George and Martha have created but by which they have been haunted. Word gives place to act, illusion to reality. Albee's own explanation of the play's title is that he derived it from a sign which he had seen in a Greenwich Village bar, and that it means, "Who's afraid of life without false illusions?"

Ostensibly a Strindbergian drama of sexual tension, in fact the play is an elaborate metaphor for what Albee sees as the willing substitution of fantasy for reality, the destructive and dangerous infantilising of the imagination and the moral being by fear. And the apocalyptic overtones of the play are deliberately underscored. The action takes place in a township called New Carthage—a Spenglerian reference underlined by George's casual reading from *The Decline of the West*, jokingly characterised by him in an early draft of the play as "a cowboy book." For Spengler, there was a clear parallel to be drawn between Carthage and modern America. In both, power and money provided the pricipal axes for behaviour. In his cyclical view of history, both marked the age of the Caesars, the victory of money power over culture. And the consequence was a brutalism and a sterile intellectualism in which "Children do not happen . . . because intelligence at the peak of intensity can no longer find any reason for their existence." And so, when George reads out the Spenglerian prophecy that "the west must . . . eventualy fall," he voices what is in effect a central thesis of the plot—a thesis underlined when George likens New Carthage to Gomorrah and Penguin Island (the latter being an island destroyed by its own capitalism in Anatole France's book of the same name), and when he suggests a parallel with Illyria—Shakespeare's fictional world.

The liberal values of the past have been willingly surrendered. George has compromised. Martha is in danger of moving "bag and baggage" into her own fantasy world. The process of the play is a slow and relentless stripping of illusion, a steady move towards the moment when their myth will collapse of its own weight, when George and Martha will be left to confront reality without benefit of their fantasies or the protective articulateness which has been their main defence. The play is, indeed, as Albee has explained more than once, "an examination of the principles of the American revolution, half tongue in cheeck, but half not." George and Martha, named after the first President and his wife, embody the fate of the American dream which has moved progressively further away from the supposed liberal idealism of those revolutionary principles.

Nick and Honey, the young people who witness the collapse of their hosts' fantasies, are themselves a warning of the next stage of decline. Honey is hopelessly timid, afraid to have children, terrified of the real. Unwilling to confront the fact that in many ways "consciousness is pain," she retreats into a childish dependence and, indeed, at one stage assumes the foetal position. Her husband, named, apparently, after Nikita Khruschev, lacks George's moral sensitivity. He is a totalitarian interested in power. In many ways he is close kin to the Young Man in *The American Dream*. He is conventionalised. Indeed, in an early version of the play he was simply to have been called "Dear." And together they have also begun to elaborate their lies. But for Albee these cannot be accurately described by Ibsen's term, "life-lies." They are, finally, destructive of life. And the hope of the play lies not simply in the process whereby George and Martha come to sacrifice their illusions and hence recover a genuine relationship with one another and with their surroundings, but also in the hope and perhaps the expectation that Nick and Honey will learn a vital lesson of the kind which Peter was presumed to derive from his experiences in *The Zoo Story*. Thus Albee has said of Nick that:

> [I]t is conceivable that there might have been some humanising going on during the course of the play to him. I don't know the extent to which Nick and Honey will be able to go on with their lives. They may have to alter a bit themselves . . . in the play all that is suggested is that you clear away all the debris and then you decide what you are going to do. It doesn't say that everything is going to be all right at all. O'Neill suggested that you have false illusions in order to survive. The only optimistic act in *Who's Afraid of Virginia Woolf?* is to say, admit that they are false illusions and then live with them if you want and know that they are false. After all, it's an act of public exorcism.

George and Martha inhabit a city of words. In recoil from reality, they laboriously construct an alternative world, lovingly elaborating their illusions in an apparently concrete language. They provide their fantasy child with an entire history, transposing a supposed genuine emotional commitment onto language which must do the work for them. They meet on a lexical battlefield. Their elaborate language games are a substitute for real contact. They are, indeed, as they explain, walking what's left of their wits. George, who has surrendered to his wife's strength and fear, who has conspired both in the creation of the child and in his own moral collapse, fights on verbally. Indeed he constantly attempts to shift affairs onto a linguistic level where he can still operate, and where, apparently, there are no consequences. But while, in one sense, to speak is to lie, in another, there is a real risk that the lexical superstructure, the crust of language, will eventually collapse of its own weight and leave them with the silence which they both fear but which may reduce them to what Pirandello once called "naked figures." Their verbalisation is indeed a response to their terror of a silence in which the real questions will assert themselves. Thus, though the play's humour functions in Henri Bergson's sense of intimidating through humiliation, it is a desperate humour (what Dostoyevski called "joking between clenched teeth") which derives from a profound anxiety. George and Martha are role-players because the role offers a retreat. They perform in front of Nick and Honey. The events have a self-consicously theatrical air. Indeed, they scarcely even need that audience. Terrified of being, they play like children (there are many references to their childishness) or like actors, and "play" becomes a central metaphor. Hence the "Fun and Games" of the first act. But, more significantly, they are retreating from reality into fiction, into self-dramatisation. And inevitably that raises questions about the function of art, and, most crucially, the status of the play in which they are themselves dramatised.

There is, perhaps, a suggestion here of self-doubt on the part of a writer who distrusts not only the devalued language of public exchange but even his own articulateness. For if the process of both *The Zoo Story* and *Who's Afraid of Virginia Woolf?* is a slow retreat from language—a suggestion that truth is pre-linguistic, that speech is designed less to communicate than to give access to power or to articulate the need to deceive (the self and others)—then his own splendid articulateness as playwright is also suspect and profoundly ambiguous. It is the kind of perception, I suspect, which led him to value the strident metaphor implicit in expressionism (in *The American Dream* and *The Sandbox*), which persuaded him to warn of the values of indirection (in *The Zoo Story*) and which, in *Tiny Alice*, was going to press him to transpose the essence of his metaphysic from a linguistic to a symbolic mode. Later still (in *Box* and *Quotations from Chairman Mao Tse-Tung*), it was to provoke an aleatory mechanism, with language being splintered into fragments, a lexical jumble designed to force the audience to recognise and re-enact the process of pattern-forming, and hence fiction-making, which lies at the heart of art and life equally, and which is the basis of an absurdity which grows out of the gulf between disorder and the persistent need for reassurance.

In *Who's Afraid of Virginia Woolf?*, however, there is nevertheless a kind of truth in language, a Freudian upsurge of the subconscious perception breaking through into the conscious world. Thus George's observation that "Martha's a devil with language" is a joke containing an element of psychological insight. And though the humour in which George and Martha excel is certainly a protective device it is also evidence of a perception of dissidence or disproportion, of that sense of the ridiculous, of which Nick and Honey are unaware.

George is a liberal who admires diversity and who, as a historian, is aware of the principles which he and his society have abrogated. In the person of Nick he comes up against a man who represents an undifferentiated future. But his own withdrawal from the world of present reality, symbolised by his retreat to this small university and to the study of history (he reads or at least pretends to read a history book during his wife's adulterous gestures towards Nick), suggests a complicity in this process. Beneath the humour is a serious fear of a fatal collapse of liberal individualism. As Jung had suggested in *The Plight of the Individual in Modern Society.*

> Under the influence of scientific assumptions, not only the psyche but the individual man and, indeed, all individual events what-soever suffer a levelling down and a process of blurring that distorts the picture of reality . . . The goal and meaning of in-dividual life (which is the only *real* life) no longer lies in individual development but in the policy of the state, which is thrust upon the individual from outside and consists in the execution of an abstract idea which ultimately tends to attract all life to itself. The individual is increasingly deprived of the moral decision as to how he should live his own life.

This is the context in which George, somewhat curiously and apparently irrelevantly, announces his determination to defend Berlin. A rhetorical gesture designed to baffle Nick, it is, in effect, a half-joking, half-serious assertion of the need to resist the totalitarian. That had been the subject of his unpublished play. *The Ice Age*, and Albee has spoken of his fascination and alarm at the apparent readiness of individuals and nations to embrace totalitarian political structures and modes of thought. And, of course, President Kennedy had made Berlin a symbol of the need to resist in his famous "Ich bin ein Berliner!" speech earlier in 1962 (the year of the play's pro-duction). George's previous failure had lain precisely in his surrender of moral conscience, his inability to acknowledge the power of abstraction, and his denial of the lessons of history. Now he has to acknowledge his role in the creation of a society which could produce Nick. He is "in" history, in the sense of being both in the history department and subject to the impact of time and process, but he "is not" history, in the sense of running the history department or acknowledging his power and responsibility to deflect the course of his society and his individual fate alike. The play does presuppose a freedom which he has willingly and perversely rejected. Its process and its theme argue the necessity to re-engage that freedom which is and must be inherently ambiguous, a freedom which enables the individual to define his own nature and to establish relationships with others, but a freedom which can be seen as synonymous with abandonment and desertion: It is a freedom, moreover, which posits no transcendence. George's respect for the aging god of the college (the president whose offer of an eventual reward has cowed him) must end. But the cost of that is to abandon the future as a compensatory mechanism; it is to inhabit the present. Buried in the play, indeed, is a metaphysical dimension which becomes more explicit in *Tiny Alice*. George and Martha are to be redeemed by the sacrifice of a son. But the gospel of love becomes a secular necessity. Vertiginous freedom has to be embraced. It is the knowledge that, in Martha's words, "You're in a straight line . . . and it doesn't lead anywhere . . . except maybe to the grave," which is the source of their terror, the ultimate reality which they would evade but must end by embracing. Denied even the vicarious survival implied by children they have to settle for the irreducible reality of an existence whose meaning has to be generated by actions taken and relationships forged.

The process of Albee's early plays tends to be a progressive stripping not only of illusions but of language. The too-ready gush of words reduces to a trickle as the characters learn to accept the reality which their articulateness is designed to deny. And the fundamental thing that they have to accept is their own mortality, the pressure of time. The denial of time is ultimately the denial of one's humanity. And so George identifies the ageless quality of the insane, who "maintain a . . . firm-skinned serenity" because "the underuse of everything leaves them quite whole." And, of course, the characters in the play are just such figures. Their baby talk, their games, their unengaged human potential, has infantilised them. Afraid of time they have become vicious Peter Pans. Nick prides himself on his detachment. George has simply compromised: "Accommodation, malleability, adjustment . . . these do seem to be the order of things." Either way, moral instincts are suppressed. Euphemism becomes a central strategy and alcohol a convenient opiate. They have suffered a "gradual . . . going to sleep of the brain cells." Afraid of pain, they retreat from consciousness into oblivion or myth. Hence, as George observes, "when people can't abide things as they are, when they can't abide the present, they do one of two things . . . either they . . . either they turn to a contemplation of the past, as I have done, or they set about to . . . alter the future." History and science, as represented by George and Nick, become forms of evasion, rationalisations. They are fictions, ways of structuring the world and experience in such a way as to deny its contingent power. So, too, is the role-playing, the theatricality in which they indulge. And this is in part the point of the various parodies in the play, of Eugene O'Neill ("Awww, 'tis the refuge we take when the unreality of the world weighs too heavy on our tiny heads") and Tennessee Williams ("Flores para los muertos," a line from *A Streetcar Named Desire* whose original title, *The Poker Night* is also invoked by Albee), two playwrights whom Albee saw as sanctioning illusion in the face of reality. And just as Williams had been drawn to Eliot's observation that human kind "Cannot bear very much reality," so Albee has George quote from the same poem ("Here we go round the mulberry bush") as he is about to destroy the illusions behind which he and Martha have hidden.

The play ends with a radically simplified language, with the simple cadence of monosyllabic question and answer. Language no longer comes between them. Neither does illusion. The fabric of their fiction has come apart. They are left only with one another, with relationship; they acknowledge the responsibility which they had previously evaded. Where once they had used the fantasy child as a means to accuse one another, now they accept their joint failure: "*We* couldn't [have any children]." As Albee comments in a stage direction, "a hint of communion in this."

The question remains, however, whether they have simply been reconciled to their own weaknesses and unrealised dreams. Eliot identifies such a state when he has one of his characters in *The Cocktail Party* (a play which has continued to haunt Albee's imagination) announce

> If that is what you wish
> I can reconcile you to the human condition,
> The condition to which some who have gone as far as you
> Have succeeded in returning. They may remember
> The vision they have had, but they cease to regret it,
> Maintain themselves by the common routine.

But Albee, like the conspirators of Eliot's play, does not predetermine the result. Thus Julia, in *The Cocktail Party*, remarks:

> We must take the risk
> All we could do was to give them the chance.
> And now, when they are stripped naked to their souls
> And can choose, whether to put on proper costumes
> Or huddle quickly into new disguises,
> They have, for the first time, somewhere to start from.

George and Martha, who once, like Eliot's character, had consoled themselves with the thought that ". . . we can fight each other, / Instead of each taking his corner of the cage" (a thought not that remote, either, from *The Zoo Story*), now have the chance to start again, as do Nick ("My God, I think I understand") and Honey.

Like *The Zoo Story*, *Who's Afraid of Virginia Woolf?* is a protest against what Albee saw as a growing conformity, a retreat from individuality and moral responsibility. It is offered not merely as an observation about human relationships but as a Catonian warning about the collapse of value in society. It stands as an assertion of the absolute need to accept responsibility for one's actions and to close the gap between individuals, to end private and public alienation. In this, Albee is in many ways close to the conviction expressed by Jung in *The Undiscovered Self*, though without Jung's faith in a transcendent dimension. In this sense George and Martha's battles become a model of social and political battles which derive from a desire to externalise and defeat qualities and tendencies inherent in the body politic. As Jung observes, "Nothing has a more divisive and alienating effect upon society than this moral complacency and lack of responsibility . . . There can be no doubt that in the democracies too the great distance between man and man is much greater than is conducive to public welfare or beneficial to our psychic needs." Human relations derive precisely from human vulnerability, from "imperfection . . . what is weak, helpless and in need of support." Nor, he insists, should such observations be seen as "superfluous sentimentalities," for "The question of human relationship and of the inner cohesion of our society is an urgent one in view of the atomization of the pent-up mass man . . . the free society needs a bond of an affective nature, a principle of a kind like *caritas*, the Christian love of your neighbour." And this is precisely the value identified by Albee. The association of *caritas* with a sexually charged relationship certainly runs the risk of sentimentality but here this is largely avoided. Albee's objection to the film version, however, lay precisely in its capitulation to this cliché. The concluding scene, filmed against the dawn of a new day, made the emphasis too clear while Albee objected both to the saccharine nature of the musical score and the virtual elimination of the political element, excluded by too great an emphasis on what Elizabeth Taylor called the "love-story" dimension. But, in fact, in an early version the play did end more positively and with a more explicit statement of the nexus between private and public terrors and consolations. George was to have remarked:

> That is, after all, the way things work . . . The balance . . .
> mutual respect through mutual terror? . . . Well, perhaps, if there

is no other way, that, at least, is a way. I wish you both well; I
fear for your headaches tomorrow, but . . . that will pass. And
I would make a suggestion to the two of you: You have within
you and between you . . . ripped out of you, maybe, and all, all
for the wrong reasons, though, who cares? . . . a possibility. Try
to . . . try to, in some way, establish basis for a legend: try to
. . . learn; I don't hold out much hope for you . . . things being
as they are . . . people . . . but, and I trust you've learned this
by now, the least, the least dishonorable failure is the only hon-
orable goal.

As a redundant summary of action and character it was deleted with some
purpose and effect but it stands as a clear statement of Albee's liberal faith
in the need to sustain the battle for selfhood.

For a number of critics the play's upbeat ending was seen as callous and
sentimental (in Yeats's sense of provoking unearned emotion). For Diana
Trilling, however, its weakness was that it posited a spiritually vacuous
existence for which there was no historical explanation and no sanction in
personal psychology. All it offered was a terrible kind of awareness. For
Harold Clurman its chief failing was that it seemed to confirm that disease—
in the sense of morbid-mindedness—could be turned into a brilliant theatrical
formula. Each, in other words, reacted against the play as though it were
an absurdist account. But in fact the historiography of betrayal is spelled
out with some care and the politics of despair located as a product of fear
and not some metaphysical determinism. The university is chosen as a setting
not out of any desire to flatter the audience (Diana Trilling suggests that
"the privileged position of Mr Albee's characters permits his audience to
identify itself with a supposedly superior class in our society") nor even
simply as a justification for an articulate debate over moral values, but because
the university is conventionally regarded as the centre of a particular kind
of freedom, as the embodiment of liberal humanist values, and hence betrayal
here is the more profound and disturbing. And far from articulateness being
presented as a virtue the process of the play exposes the degree to which it
may be the root of a crucial act of evasion, and intelligence, drained of human
purpose, a threat to survival. It is possible to see the final tableau as sentimental. Restored personal relationships are made to carry the weight of the
play's allegorical meaning. But in a sense it is the very fragility of that new
structure which inhibits a complete collapse into the dubious sexual metaphysics of Tennessee Williams's *The Rose Tattoo* or *Period of Adjustment*. Nothing is certain. The fear remains: what has gone is the elaborate structure of
illusion. They can never simply fall into such a strategy again. Like Peter

in *The Zoo Story*, if they are to revert to their old habits it must at the very least be a willed and knowing acknowledgment of defeat.

In a sense Albee's early plays read like a pastiche of Martin Buber and Erich Fromm, both popular figures in the late 1950s and early 1960s. They address the question of alienation, an alienation which is partly a product of capitalism and partly an aspect of what it was then popular to call the human condition. A classic statement of this is to be found in Erich Fromm's *The Sane Society:*

> Man is torn away from the primary union with nature, which characterizes animal existence. Having at the same time reason and imagination, he is aware of his aloneness and separateness; of his powerlessness and ignorance; of the accidentalness of his birth and of his death. He could not face this state of being for a second if he could not find new ties with his fellow man which replace the old ones, regulated by instincts. Even if all his physiological needs were satisfied, he would experience his state of aloneness and individuation as a prison from which he had to break out in order to retain his sanity . . . There is only one passion which satisfies man's need to unite himself with the world, and to acquire at the same time a sense of integrity and individuality, and this is love.

But under the conditions of modern society men become "atoms . . . little particles estranged from each other" so that "the drive for exchange operates and *All Over*, strikes at the essence of identity and meaning alike. The failure of these characters lies in their tendency to opt for fantasy rather than imagination; the one substitutes, the other is generative. George and Martha's child is fantasy. Their relationship at the end of the play, the moment of fragile contact at the end of *The Zoo Story*, requires an imaginative perception, a glimpse of the mutuality which constitutes the only resource available.

Lionel Trilling has said that "all literature tends to be concerned with the question of reality. I mean quite simply the old opposition between reality and appearance, between what really is and what merely seems." And certainly Albee has concerned himself directly with this subject. But where in the early plays he tended to accept a simple opposition such as that identified by Trilling—that is, he accepted a fundamentally liberal view of art as being concerned with identifying a reality which is at base easily perceived if painfully acknowledged (moral sense being in some way identical with common sense)—in his subsequent work things seem less clear. Increasingly he has become concerned with the question of the nature of the real, and this has inevitably led him to a consideration of the nature of theatre. The Aristotelian position has increasingly been deserted for a more complex consideration. And his own theatrical experimentation became more radical, his next play being produced not on Broadway but in a small theatre in Buffalo—a displaced version of Off-Broadway.

Box and *Quotations from Chairman Mao Tse-Tung* (1968) reflect Albee's sense of diminishing possibilities and his perception of a shift, if not in American values, then in the possibility of those values acting as transforming mechanisms. Looking back, in the late 1970s, to the beginning of his career he observed that, "Ater all, Kennedy was not dead yet. The war in Vietnam had not convinced us that as a society we were capable of cynical politics. A number of things had not happened at that point." Accordingly, he confessed that

> It may be that I am becoming less and less certain about the resiliency of civilisation. Maybe I am becoming more and more depressed by the fact that I don't think people want to make the dangerous experiment. People desire to live as dictatorships tell them to do. There is a totalitarian impulse . . . I suppose [this] comes from watching carefully what has been going on. After all, I would like to think that I still write out of a certain amount of anger and contempt. I don't think that has changed very much. The nature of the anger may have changed.

In *Box*, Albee pushes the logic of his warnings one final stage further. He creates a post-apocalyptic elegy, a theatre without characters because it is an attempt to project the destructive tendencies of society to their ultimate conclusions. It is both a warning and a threnody. The stage is dominated by the outlined frame of a cube. No actors appear; we simply hear the monologue of a middle-aged woman whose tones are deliberately flattened so as to make it difficult to relate her to any particular locality. Her observations seem to refer to some calamity which may already have happened (the past tense predominates), thereby explaining a world bereft of people and represented by a box which may stand as an image of a coffin. There is, strictly speaking, no time. The play takes place in that timeless moment identified by Eliot in "The Hollow Men," between the "idea" and the "reality," the "essence" and the "descent." And the stuttering conclusion of that poem is in essence equally that of Albee's play:

> For Thine is
> Life is

> For Thine is the
> This is the way the world ends
> This is the way the world ends
> This is the way the world ends
> Not with a bang but a whimper.

Albee's play ends like this:

> Nothing belongs
> (Three second silence. Great sadness)
> Look; more of them; a black net . . . skimming
> (Pause)
> And just one . . . moving beneath . . . in the opposite way
> (Three second silence. Very sad, supplicating)
> Milk
> (Three second silence)
> Milk
> (Five second silence. Wistful)
> Box
> (Silence, except for the sound of bell buoys and sea gulls. Very
>   slow fading of lights to black, sound of bell buoys and
>   sea gulls fading with the light.)

The explosion which is envisaged as a constant possibility and which is finally only confirmation of a more fundmental collapse of morale and morality has perhaps already happened. The milk of human kindness is as contaminated as is the literal milk by radioactivity. The centre cannot hold. Albee, too, is a poet of the hollow men.

It is [as] though we had caught just the final instant, without time to relate the event to its environment—the thing happening to the thing happened to. The fact that *Box* was designed to be played before and after its companion piece, *Quotations*, suggests its role as warning and epitaph, an indictment not only of a society and a race but of an art which has compounded the destructive values which it should have denounced.

In an introduction Albee proposes the twin obligations of the writer: "to make some statement about the condition of 'man' (as it is put) and, second to make some statement about the nature of the art form with which he is working. In both instances he must attempt change . . . The playwright must try to alter his society," and "since art must move, or wither—the playwright must try to alter the forms within which his precursors have had to work." *Box*, however, poses the question in a more subtle form. What exactly is the function of art in a period in which history is perceived as an implacable force, in which the logic of technology has replaced morality and hence the efficacy of that art? And so the disembodied voice identifies the world of "system as conclusion, in the sense of method as an end, the dice so big you can hardly throw them any more," a world in which "progress is merely a direction, movement," and suggests that the inevitable consequence of this inhuman logic, given an accompanying apathy, is "seven hundred million babies dead in the time it takes, took, to knead the dough to make a proper loaf." Given this reality "little wonder so many . . . went . . . cut off, said no instead of hanging on." The spiritual death which his earlier plays had identified and deplored is now seen as in part a response to a threatened apocalypse, as it had been in *The Death of Bessie Smith*, its "great, red-orange-yellow sunset" like a fire enveloping half of the continent, and *Who's Afraid of Virginia Woolf?*, with its reference to Gomorrah and Penguin Island.

The voice recalls a time "when it was *simple*," a world which, in theatrical terms, could adequately be represented by realism as a style, in which the individual was assumed to bear the imprint of social forces and the meticulous reproduction of detail offered a clue to public and private realities. And thus the large wooden cube, which is the only object on the stage, becomes an image on the one hand of a classical symmetry and on the other of a fastidious form, a well-made art work—a *pièce bien fait*. But such art, it is suggested, failed to warn of a fatal cancer. It implied order and control. In offering to mimic life it reflected back its own coherences to a world which otherwise was without them. The function of art, the voice implies, should have been to warn rather than to console. And so the voice laments, "If only they had *told* us! Clearly! When it was clear that we were not only corrupt—for there is nothing that is not, or little—but corrupt to the selfishness, to the corruption that we should die to keep it." For the fear is that it "gets to a certain point" when "the momentum is too much." The empty stage is the primary evidence for that.

A process which begins with "the *little* things, the *small* cracks," eventually destroys the organism. And the function of art becomes not the pursuit of beauty but the necessity to remind us of loss, for "When art begins to hurt, it's time to look around." But the problem is that art inevitably cauterises the very wounds which it opens up insofar as it implies order, consonance, coherence. It is potentially trapped in falsification. And to attempt to break out of the paradox is to create an art which does not present itself in Arnoldian terms, which is not "a matter of garden, or straight lines, or even . . . morality." But this is to risk breaking free equally of those for whom it is designed; "and they say, what is *that?*"—an experience not un-known to Albee. Compromises have to be made: "we give up something." The writer's responsibility may, in one of the play's more striking images, be to be the one bird flying in one direction while a billion fly the other way (Albee once described the writer's function to be "out-of-step" with his society) but, if there is no communication, there is no purpose. The awareness of loss has to be communicated if a greater loss is to be prevented. However, that possibility has seemingly disappeared, for the fatal loss is internal and spiritual: "we all died when we were thirty once. Now, much younger. Much."

Box, then, is narrated as though the bomb had already dropped, as though it were the recorded voice of an extinct race. But an ambiguity is retained. Since the play takes place in the timeless world between the striking of the chord and its resolution, the breaking of the bone and the pain, "It was the memory of it, to be seen and proved later . . . The memory of what we have not yet known." Just as with other things which we have not seen but know to be true, this account has the truth of inevitability. Because, of course, by the nature of things if this play were in fact a product of a post-apocalyptic world it could never be written, performed or observed. *Box* is, therefore, an anticipated elegy of something that "can happen here, I guess. But unprovable. Ahhhhh. That makes the difference, does it *not*. Nothing can seep here except the memory of what I'll not prove." And yet we are asked to assume that in a sense it has happened. It is like the voice of a time traveller who has seen the future and whose apocalyptic message is confirmed by the fact that the processes which will lead to that future can already be observed. Thus the other implications of the box on the bare stage become apparent. It is indeed a coffin as it is also an image of art devolved into mere craft. It is a symbol of the stage (the box stage) and beyond that of the auditorium and the theatre in which the audience already sits entombed. And yet, contradictorily, we are to presume that the writer, flying in the face of social and artistic convention, believes that even now some pre-emptive action is possible. The presumption exists in the fact of the play—a warning implies the possibility of action—but scarcely in its imagery or its language. The flaw is that the individual moral sensibility which sets the stone of history rolling is not presented as rectifiable, within the play, only as recognisable for what it is by those about to be crushed by it.

Albee's imaginative perception outstrips his moral will. The values which he appears to endorse have been evacuated from the play along with virtually everything else. We are asked by implication to reconstitute those absent values as a means to forestall the apocalypse. But the moral sensibility which this expectation implies on the part of the audience already represents a weakness in the rigour of his logic. For there are, then, it appears, still those who perceive the danger and can move to obviate it. And they are, firstly, the percipient and humane dramatist and, secondly, his sensitive and appreciative audience. Quite how this comfortable partnership has managed to remain immune to the general moral and spiritual decline is never made clear. But that it does so is a basic assumption of most, though not quite all, of his work.

Quotations from Chairman Mao Tse-Tung is a natural companion piece to *Box*. It takes place within the confines of the cube. There are four characters, only one of whom speaks lines written by Albee. One, a minister, remains silent throughout; a second, an Old Lady, recites a sentimental poem by the nineteenth-century American poet, Will Carleton; the third is Chairman Mao Tse-Tung, who literally recites from that familiar text of 1960s radicalism, the little red book containing the sayings of Chairman Mao. Each character is trapped inside his or her own experience. They occupy the same space but share nothing. Only the fourth character, the Long-Winded Lady, speaks Albee's lines and she offers a somewhat gnomic account of the decline of her own life, a decline which evidently took literal form when she plunged from the deck of an ocean liner into the sea. Indeed the connection between all the monologues is, once again, a sense of loss and impending apocalypse. But no one account is allowed to dominate. Indeed the separate narratives are themselves deliberately disrupted. Though originally written out in separate and continuous form, they were subsequently intercut with one another. The objective was, in some sense, as Albee has explained in a note to the published text, to arrive at a "musical structure—form and counterpoint," and certainly his punctuation is offered as a kind of musical notation. But beyond this the deliberate disruption of the narrative thrust has two central effects. It creates new meanings by juxtaposition, and it makes it impossible to reconstruct the individual texts with any clarity. The consequence is an aleatory effect as the audience is forced to re-enact the process of imposing order on disparate experience, which is in fact one of the subjects of the play itself.

Sometimes the effect is deliberately ironic. Following Chairman Mao's insistence that "The communist ideological and social system alone is full of youth and vitality, sweeping the world with the momentum of an avalanche and the force of a thunderbolt," the Long-Winded Lady replies "Exactly: plut!" Sometimes the voices appear to confirm one another with more conviction. But the intrusion of the voice from *Box* is a constant ironic reminder of the logic of their separate positions. And when the Long-Winded

Lady speaks of the process of decline, "sun . . . haze . . . mist . . . deep night . . . all the Spectrum down. Something Burning," the apocalyptic implications are clear. As she asks, "How many are expecting it!?"

The dominant image is entropic. Although Albee scrupulously quotes directly from Mao there is a crucial omission from one quoation, a simile which offers a clue to the connecting tissue which Albee plainly believes to exist between the private and public world. "The ideological and social system of capitalism," Mao had observed in the omitted passage, "resembles a dying person who is sinking fast, like the sun setting beyond the western hills." The Long-Winded Lady is just such a person; and she describes a literal sinking which plainly stands as an apt image of the decline of her own life—as it does of the old woman in the Carleton poem who goes "Over the Hill to the Poorhouse" as a result of the callousness of her own family and of the world in which she moves. As the voice of *Box* reminds us, insinuating its way into *Quotations*, "It's the *little* things, the *small* cracks." A failure of humanity on the personal scale is essentially of the same kind as, and, indeed, may have a causative relationship to, the failure of humanity on a national scale.

And the illusions treasured and propounded by all of the characters— religious, political, sexual—are presented not merely as being similarly destructive but as stemming from a similar impulse. The influence here seems to be that of Freud who, in *The Future of an Illusion*, had said,

> man cannot remain a child for ever; he must venture at last into the hostile world. This may be called *"education* to *reality."*

Albee's work has always been dedicated to precisely this process; while *Quotations from Chairman Mao Tse-Tung* would seem to be a literal enactment of Freud's observation that

> having recognised religious doctrines to be illusions, we are at once confronted with the further question: may not other cultural possessions, which we esteem highly and by which we let our life be ruled, be of a similar nature? Should not the assumptions that regulate our political institutions likewise be called illusions, and is it not the case that in our culture the relations between the sexes are disturbed by an erotic illusion, or by a series of erotic illusions?

Albee has insisted that both of these related plays "deal with the unconscious, primarily," and by this he seems to mean both the degree to which they suggest that all dimensions of human life—private, social and metaphysical—

are an expression of a need which can hardly be articulated or apprehended, and that it is only on the level of the unconscious that the fragmented components of his theme can cohere. Thus the plays become less something to be consciously analysed, than an experience to which the audience is invited to submit itself. The fear to which he addresses himself and the need which generates the action exist at a level beneath that susceptible of rational analysis. And the unconscious, as the seat of the imagination, also represents the possible source of redemption. As the Long-Winded Lady remarks, "if we control the conscious, we're either mad or . . . dull witted."

On one level the characters can be seen as representing the past (the Old Lady), present (Long-Winded Lady) and future (Mao), or the personal and public dimensions of human failure. The silence of the minister certainly implies his irrelevance. God is plainly dead or indifferent. And the consequence is a destructive solipsism. On another level the characters are simply fictionalised forms controlled partly by the manipulative imagination of the writer and partly by chance. Dislodged from their contexts they are drained equally of their original function and meaning. Experience, and, indeed, language, are thus exposed as arbitrary and plastic. All that remains is a consistency of imagery, a disruption of harmony, which the play's form mimics. The characters' separate accounts are dominated by the notion of space—the space between meaning and language, between family and social group, between the self and its experience. Decline is the only constant, death the logical conclusion of all narratives. But Albee has insisted that even here, in a play which he agrees is concerned with a series of alternative fictions, there remains a moral intent, suggesting that it "offers cautionary tales about most of the characters of a certain age, and people who are still capable of change but are also capable of avoiding it." The moral world, we must presume, is projected beyond the text. It is certainly not contained within it. But, for all his insistence on the moral force of the play, it effectively evades his control. All he feels able to assert is the need not to compound the absurdity which is a product of decline and death, not to anticipate it. Thus the Long-Winded Lady describes an occasion on which she had broken her thumb and screamed before the pain had resulted. "Before the hurt could have gone through, I made it happen. Well; we do that . . . Yes, we do that: we make it happen a little before it need."

For Albee, there is a crucial distinction to be made between Mao, "who published his thoughts and didn't change his mind," the Old Lady, "who is reciting Over the Hill to the Poorhouse and whose lines are determined," the minister who "naturally says absolutely nothing," and the Long-Winded Lady who "is the only one character who is capable of change." He has insisted that "she constantly startled me. I knew exactly what the others were going to say. They didn't surprise me at all." The problem is that while he insists that she is capable of change there is little evidence for this within the play.

For Mao, the socialist system is "an objective law independent of man's will," and history an implacable force. It leaves no more space for identity to cohere, for the individual to locate a personal and public meaning, than did the capitalist enterprise parodied by the nineteenth-century poem and exposed by the Long-Winded Lady's tale of alienation and despair, or the now impotent and mute religious determinisms. The need to submit oneself to totalitarian ideas, to religious ideals, to public myths of progress, stems, he implies, less from their self-evident logic than from a desperate need for order. After all, if everything is regarded as "part of a . . . predetermination, or something that had already happened in principle—well, under *those* conditions *any* chaos becomes order. Any chaos at all." And this incubus, of course, exists no less among the members of the audience, concerned with identifying the "meaning" of the play which they are watching and desperately rearranging the fragments to reconstitute a whole which at the very least can make sense of their decision to spend $20 and an hour of their time. The conviction that a plan exists seems the unavoidable condition of art— an implied contract with the audience. It is the paradox which Albee tries to tackle, though it must be said that he tries to have his philosophical cake and eat it.

In a sense the problem which the play poses is that offered by those *trompe-l'œil* pictures in which two images coexist but which the eye can only perceive individually. The patterns which constitute one shape disrupt those which form another. To reconstitute the monologues of *Quotations* is, unavoidably, to destroy the assonances which derive from the juxtaposition of the fragments. The various realities coexist as do the characters themselves. Albee's equivocation lies in the fact that he himself wishes to locate an underlying structure, suggesting that the play is about the necessity for change. This would be a fair description of most of his work; it is singularly inappropriate to this play which dramatises a series of closed systems, occupying the same space but independent of one another. Albee's comments notwithstanding, there is no suggestion that any of the characters is capable of change. History, art and an ineluctable egotism are too powerful to brook any dissent. The dislocations of the text are in effect those of the private and public world; they dramatise that lack of social or moral cohesiveness which is a distinguishing characteristic of the world which he pictures. The young are presented, both in the Old Lady's recitation and the Long-Winded

Lady's monologue, as intensely selfish and unavoidably brutal. And the same logic which makes possible the collapse of love and concern in the family, the remarkable transmutation of love into hate or indifference, draws the race towards the annihilation promised by Mao. Totalitarianism of the self is presented as being of a piece with political totalitarianism, and the alliance with death embodied in the betrayals of love on a private level has its parallel and logical consequence in the ultimate apocalypse of nuclear warfare. The image of that final willed suicide runs throughout a play which in effect offers an eschatology of the modern age. In a world in which, as the voice of Box interjects, "nothing belongs" (an echo of O'Neill) there is no longer any force to hold the pieces together except the imagination, but, as the Long-Winded Lady admits "one's imagination . . . is poor support."

Albee has found himself enrolled in a number of public causes most especially that of dissident writers. He has commented on the plight of the artist in South Korea and in Czechoslovakia. And it is no accident that he should have chosen to concentrate on the artist for, to his mind, he is a crucial figure. Whether in a totalitarian country or in one in which consensus politics and a bland materialism define the norm, the writer is seen as representing and defining a form of freedom. The imagination creates the possibility of alternatives while the circumstances of drama in particular establish the collective nature of experience and thereby the necessity for a system of moral responsibility. As he has said:

> I find very little difference between such a closed society as the Soviet Union and an open society such as ours. In a theoretically classless society such as the Soviet Union the arts are controlled from the top, while in the United States, this theoretically corrupt, heavily classed, society, the arts are controlled by the people. It is unhealthy for the arts to exist in a society where the minds of the people are controlled from the top by bureaucrats and it is not terribly healthy for the arts to have to exist in a society of the commodity market. But I have noticed that in closed societies, where people are not allowed to have access to the metaphor, there are brave people who want access to the metaphor and will gain it at whatever cost. While in a society where there is nobody stopping free access to the metaphor we are indifferent to the treasure of the metaphor.

For Albee this process is fundamental to the playwright's art. He also said, "I think a person is born a playwright or a painter because it's a way of responding to reality, to outside stimuli and then translating them into something else." In a sense all theatre is metaphorical in that an actor's actions stand for those of a character but Albee's drama is metaphorical in another sense. His plays offer a series of allegories. Despite his denials, he is a didactic writer and his theatre a teaching mechanism. It poses questions whose answers may not lie within the work of art itself. A communal mode, it demonstrates the individual's reliance on others for the generation of meaning; a public art, it relies on the reality of shared experience for its effect. Albee's realism is charged with metaphysics, his metaphysics constrained by his liberal humanism. He began his career as a "demonic social critic," recalling America to its liberal principles and he remains that, though America has changed and he himself has lost some confidence in the ability of art to oppose the move towards apocalypse.

> I don't necessarily like the environment in which playwrights have to work in this society of ours. Not only the environment in which playwrights have to work but that in which all creative people have to work—novelists, poets, sculptors, painters. Why should anyone bother to concern himself with the state of the arts in their society? Have we not had a rough time in the last fifteen years? Have we not had a war in Vietnam which tore our society apart? Have we not seen students shot down on campus, clubbed? Haven't we seen our economy in a shambles? Haven't we seen the presidency disgraced? We've had quite a bit to concern us, things of some magnitude. But, in the face of all this, art remains of central importance . . . We are the only animal which consciously creates art, attempts metaphor. It is our distinguishing mark . . . if we turn out to be the kind of society which is unwilling to use the metaphor, to use art to instruct us about ourselves, then we are a society which is on its way downhill without ever having seen the top. Indeed if we are unwise enough not to be instructed by the arts then perhaps we do lack the will, the wisdom, the courage, to support a free society.

The logic that he identifies in *Box* and *Quotations from Chairman Mao Tse-Tung* may have suggested silence as the only means to avoid collusion with the forces of death but to Albee such a silence would have constituted a final betrayal, a collaboration more total than that risked by the deployment of metaphors deeply ambiguous in their origin and profoundly disturbing in their effect.

MATTHEW C. ROUDANÉ

The Man Who Had Three Arms

In *The Man Who Had Three Arms*, which opened October 4, 1982, at the Goodman Theatre in Chicago (it had its New York debut at the Lyceum in the spring of 1983), the protagonist, Himself, launches a verbal attack, not on an unsuspecting Peter, a bewildered Nick and Honey, an anesthetized Tobias, or a retiring Charlie, but on his audience. Savagely divided against self and world, Himself berates the audience in a desperate attempt to come to terms with the incubi haunting his soul: his undeserved fame and subsequent fall from stardom. Apparently the confluence of the public exposure and the private tensions within Himself explains his militant attitude toward the audience.

It is a Pirandellian audience, of course. That is, *The Man Who Had Three Arms* quickly establishes itself as a metatheatrical experience: the play blatantly insists upon its artificiality, simultaneously calling attention to its own language and exposing the meaninglessness of that language. The audience is both the imaginary group of listeners attending the "Man on Man" lecture series and the actual theatergoers. Himself's hostile account of his sudden celebrity when he mysteriously grew a third arm and of his equally abrupt fall from fame when the arm disappeared embodies Albee's thematic concerns and aesthetic theories regarding the civic function of drama.

Similarly, the stage directions signal multiple roles for Man and Woman, the other two characters in the play. They become, at one point, a physician and a nurse whose comments complement Himself's account of the medical world's reaction to his third appendage. Earlier, when Himself mocks the

---

From *Understanding Edward Albee*. © 1987 by the University of South Carolina Press.

Catholic Church, the Man appears as a priest and accuses the speaker, "You are a freak of nature," With deliberate self-consciousness, the Man and the Woman call attention to the rhetorical gallantries—and artificiality—of their introductory exchange:

> WOMAN: . . . Dear friends, we *have* been fortunate over the
>   years, being witness, as we have, to those who have made
>   our history and shaped our culture, men and women
>   whose accomplishments have wreaked their order on our
>   havoc.
> MAN: Oh! What a very nice phrase!
> WOMAN: *(Genuinely pleased):* Thank you, *thank* you!
> *(To her notes again)* . . . their order on our havoc and identified
>   our reality by creating it for us.
> MAN: Even better! *(Begins applauding)* My goodness.

Albee's Pirandellian technique functions on two important levels. First, such a technique invites the audience to question its willing suspension of disbelief. By calling attention to the very nature of theatricality, Albee experiments with the illusion of dramatic mimesis, challenging traditional responses. Second, like *Six Characters in Search of an Author*, *The Man Who Had Three Arms* forces the audience to break down the barrier between itself and the actors. However, in *The Man Who Had Three Arms*, Albee minimizes the barrier radically, involving the audience directly as participants throughout the action. At one point Himself talks to the audience, with the stage directions and dialogue suggesting the intimacy between the actor and spectator. Albee permits a degree of directorial freedom within parts of the text:

> (To someone in the front) Do you remember what I said? Before
> we broke? Remember I said that if you came upon me sobbing
> in a corner, not to disturb? That it was a way I had and not to
> worry? Do you remember? *(Note: If the person says "yes," say: "You
> do!" If person says "no," say: "You don't!" If person fails to respond,
> wing it, choosing what you like.)*

Albee does not direct the actor to start fighting with the actual audience, as Julian Beck had members of *The Living Theatre* do. Still, Albee creates an overly aggressive text, expanding the boundaries of theater as collective, communal spectacle. Discussing this point, he considers the relatedness of the actors and audience within his theory of drama:

> I don't like the audience as voyeur, the audience as passive spec-
> tator. I want the audience as participant. In that sense, I agree

with Artaud: that sometimes we should literally draw blood. I am very fond of doing that because voyeurism in the theater lets people off the hook. *The Man Who Had Three Arms* is a specific attempt to do this. It is an act of aggression. It's probably the most violent play I've written.

The play's fictional and actual audience, for better or worse, stands as the recipient of the violence. But as in all of Albee's theater, the violence is more metaphysical and psychological than physical. Moments into the play, Himself chides the audience, but the sarcasm quickly modulates to verbal assault:

> *(Looking across the front row)* Where is she? Where is she, I wonder; the lady, the girl, usually, who sits there in the front row, almost *always*, wherever, whenever I speak—not the *same* girl, woman, you understand, but of a certain type: plain, more than a little overweight, smock top, jeans, sandals, dirty toenails—sits there in the front row, and, as I lecture, *try* to lecture, try to fill you in, so to speak, make you understand, sits there and runs her tongue around her open mouth, like this, *(Demonstrates)* hand in her crotch, likely as not, bitten fingers, lascivious, obscene, does it over and over, all through my lecture, my expiation, my sad, sad tale, unnerves me, bores, finally wearies me with her longing.

Act 2 begins with a tale hat escalates Himself's attack on the audience. Himself claims to have assaulted a female journalist who hounded him during intermission, although Albee presents the account ambiguously enough so that the viewer is never sure whether it actually happened.

> "You're good," she said, "you're really good." There was a loathing to it, a condemnation that I dare be articulate, coherent. "You're really good." "So are you," I said. "You've got balls."

> The energy of the hatred here, the mutual rage and revulsion was such that, had we fucked, we would have shaken the earth with our cries and thumps and snarls and curses: a crashing around of Gods—chewed nipples, bleeding streaks along the back. Had we fucked . . . Oh, Jesus! what issue! *But* . . . but the only issue was the issue of me, the . . . dismemberment of me. "You've got balls!" I said. And I crashed my hand into her crotch like a goosing twelve-year-old. "Get your hands off me," she said. "Get your filthy hands off me." I withdrew my hand:

it had hit rock. "If you'll excuse me," she said, ice, shoving past me. She is an impressive lady.

In his monologue of cruelty, then, Himself not only chronicles the growth of his third arm and its cataclysmic effect on his world but implicates the audience throughout for contributing to his present condition. Once a freakish cultural icon, he is now a grotesque, groveling figure. His lecture represents his last pathetic connection with a public he both needs and abhors.

Throwing over the podium, Himself closes the play with a loving plea to the audience to stay, a hateful cry to leave, a pitiful gesture to understand:

> No one leaves until you apologize to me!! I want an apology for all the years!! For all the humiliation!! *(Sudden change of tone; abrupt realization of futility; a great weariness)* Nah! You don't owe me anything. Get out of here! Leave me alone! Leave me alone! *(Curtain starts; Himself notices.) (Off)* No! Don't do that! Don't leave me alone! *(Out)* Stay with me. Don't . . . leave me alone! Don't leave me! Don't . . . leave me alone. *(Curtain completes itself.)*

In theory and structure, in language and theme, *The Man Who Had Three Arms* boldly attempts to extend the conventions of the contemporary theater. The play stands as testimony to Albee's ongoing willingness to experiment with text and performance, without regard to commercial pressures. But while he certainly succeeds in fulfilling one of his central goals—to involve the audience as active participants—Albee may lose the real audience he needs in the first place. The play does not sustain the dramaturgic burdens the author places on it. *The Man Who Had Three Arms* does not shock the audience into the self-awareness that we sense at the close of *The Zoo Story*, nor the catharsis we experience at the climax of *Who's Afraid of Virginia Woolf?*.

Chronology

1928   Born March 12 in Washington, D.C. Adopted at two weeks of age by millionaire Reed Albee and his wife, Frances. Named for his adoptive grandfather, Edward Franklin Albee, partner in Keith-Albee Theater Circuit.

1940   Attends Lawrenceville School. Writes three-act play, *Aliqueen*.

1943   Dismissed from Lawrenceville. Attends Valley Forge Military Academy; subsequently dismissed.

1944   Attends Choate School.

1945   Writes poem entitled "Eighteen," which is published in *Kaleidograph*, a Texas literary magazine.

1946   *Schism*, his first published play, appears in *Choate Literary Magazine*. Writes a novel and some poetry.

1947   Leaves Trinity College, Hartford, during his second year and writes for music programming on WNYC radio.

1948–58   Lives in Greenwich Village on the proceeds of grandmother's trust fund, supplemented by a series of odd jobs.

1958   In the course of three weeks writes *The Zoo Story*, first produced in Berlin, September 1959.

1960   First American production of *The Zoo Story*, Provincetown Playhouse, New York. *The Death of Bessie Smith*, Berlin; *The Sandbox*, New York; *Fam and Yam*, Westport, Connecticut.

1961   *The American Dream*, with *The Death of Bessie Smith*, New York. *Bartleby*, an operatic adaptation of Melville's short story (written in collaboration with William Flanagan), is poorly received and withdrawn.

1962   *Who's Afraid of Virginia Woolf?*, New York. Its nomination for the Pulitzer Prize is not accepted unanimously by the committee, and two members of the drama subcommittee resign. Receives New York Drama Critics Award and Tony Award.

1963   *The Ballad of the Sad Café* (adaptation from Carson McCullers), New York.

1964   *Tiny Alice*, New York.

1966   *Malcolm* (adaptation of novel by James Purdy), New York; closes after five days. *A Delicate Balance*, New York, for which he wins Pulitzer Prize.

1967   *Everything in the Garden* (adaptation of play by Giles Cooper), New York.

1968   *Box* and *Quotations from Chairman Mao Tse-Tung*, Buffalo Studio Arena Theater.

1971   *All Over*, New York.

1975   *Seascape*, New York, for which he wins Pulitzer Prize.

1977   *Counting the Ways* and *Listening* (appeared first as radio play in 1976 in England).

1980   *The Lady from Dubuque.*

1981   *Lolita* (adaptation of the novel by Vladimir Nabokov).

1983   *The Man Who Had Three Arms*, New York.

Contributors

HAROLD BLOOM, Sterling Professor of the Humanities at Yale University, is the author of *The Anxiety of Influence, Poetry and Repression*, and many other volumes of literary criticism. His forthcoming study, *Freud: Transference and Authority*, attempts a full-scale reading of all of Freud's major writings. A MacArthur Prize Fellow, he is general editor of five series of literary criticism published by Chelsea House.

BRIAN WAY is the author of *Audience Participation: Theatre for Young People* and *Development through Drama*, as well as studies of F. Scott Fitzgerald and Herman Melville.

GERALD WEALES is Professor of English at the University of Pennsylvania and the author of *American Drama Since World War II, Religion in Modern Drama, A Play and Its Parts, The Jumping-Off Place*, and *Tale for the Bluebird*, a novel.

PAUL WITHERINGTON is Associate Professor of English at South Dakota State University and has written on Emily Dickinson, Melville, and Crane, in addition to Albee.

RONALD HAYMAN is the author of *Literature and Living: A Reconsideration of Katherine Mansfield and Virginia Woolf, The Set-Up: An Anatomy of the English Theatre Today, How To Read a Play, Theatre and Anti-Theatre*, and *K., a Biography of Kafka*, as well as full-length studies of Albee, Arden, Artaud, Beckett, Bolt, Brecht, Fassbinder, Ionesco, Arthur Miller, Nietzsche, John Osborne, Pinter, de Sade, Stoppard, Tolstoy, Arnold Wesker, and John Whiting, among others.

ANTHONY HOPKINS teaches English at Glendon College, York University, and has written on film and popular culture, as well as modern drama.

MARY CASTIGLIE ANDERSON is Assistant Professor of English at Lyman Briggs College/Michigan State University.

JULIAN N. WASSERMAN is Professor of English at Loyola University and co-author of *The Poetics of Conversion: Numerology and Alchemy in Gottfried's Tristan* and *Thomas Hardy and the Tristan Legend.*

LIAM O. PURDON is Assistant Professor of English and American Literature at Doane College at Crete, Nebraska.

THOMAS P. ADLER is Professor of English at Purdue University, specializing in drama.

C. W. E. BIGSBY is Reader in the School of English and American Studies at the University of East Anglia. He has edited *Superculture* and *Approaches to Popular Culture* and is the author of *Confrontation and Commitment*, *Dada and Surrealism*, and *Tom Stoppard*, among other books.

MATTHEW C. ROUDANÉ edits *Studies in the Literary Imagination* and teaches in the Department of English at Georgia State University. He is the author of a number of articles and a forthcoming book on Edward Albee.

Bibliography

Adler, Thomas P. "Albee's *Seascape:* Humanity and the Second Threshold." *Renascence* 31 (1978): 107–14.

Ballew, Leighton M. "Who's Afraid of *Tiny Alice?*" *Georgia Review* 20 (1966): 292–99.

Baxandall, Lee. "The Theatre of Edward Albee," *Tulane Drama Review* 9 (1965): 19–40.

Bennett, Robert B. "Tragic Vision in *The Zoo Story.*" *Modern Drama* 20 (1977): 55–66.

Bierhaus, E. G., Jr. "Strangers in a Room: *A Delicate Balance* Revisited." *Modern Drama* 17 (1973): 199–206.

Bigsby, C. W. E. "Edward Albee." In *Confrontation and Commitment*, 71–92. London: MacGibbon & Kee, 1967.

———. *Edward Albee*. Edinburgh: Oliver & Boyd, 1969.

———. *Edward Albee: A Collection of Critical Essays*. Englewood Cliffs, N. J.: Prentice-Hall, 1975.

Blum, Harold. "A Psychoanalytic View of *Who's Afraid of Virginia Woolf?*" In *Lives, Events, and Other Players: Directions in Psychobiography*, 271–83. New York: Aronson, 1981.

Brustein, Robert. *Seasons of Discontent*. New York: Simon & Schuster, 1965.

Campbell, Mary Elizabeth. "The Tempters in Albee's *Tiny Alice.*" *Modern Drama* 13 (1969): 22–33.

Cardullo, B. "Pinter's *The Homecoming* and Albee's *A Delicate Balance.*" *The Explicator* 42 (1984): 54–56.

Carr, Duane R. "St. George and the Snapdragons: The Influence of Unamuno on *Who's Afraid of Virginia Woolf?*" *Arkansas Quarterly* 29 (1972): 5–13.

Chester, Alfred. "Edward Albee: Red Herring and White Whales." *Commentary* 35 (1963): 296–301.

Ciuba, Gary M. "Albee's Descent of Man: Generational Conflict and Evolutionary Change." *Mid-Hudson Language Studies* 6 (1983): 73–9.

Debusscher, Gilbert. *Edward Albee: Tradition and Renewal*. Brussels: American Studies Center, 1967.

Downer, Alan S., ed. "An Interview with Edward Albee." In *The American Theater*, 123–36. Washington: USIS, 1967.

Ducker, Dan " 'Pow!' 'Snap!' 'Pouf!': The Modes of Communication in *Who's Afraid of Virginia Woolf?*" *CIA Journal* 26 (1983): 465–77.

Dukore, Bernard F. "A Warp in Albee's Woolf." *Southern Speech Journal* 30 (1965): 261–68.

Duplessis, Rachel Blau. "In the Bosom of the Family: Contradiction and Resolution in Edward Albee." *Minnesota Review* 8 (1976): 133–45.

Esslin, Martin. *The Theatre of the Absurd.* New York: Doubleday, 1961.

Flanagan, William. "Edward Albee." In *Writers at Work*, 321–46. New York: Viking, 1967.

Flash, Mrs. Harold A. "Games People Play in *Who's Afraid of Virginia Woolf?*" *Modern Drama* 10 (December 1967): 280–88.

Fletcher, John. " 'A Psychology Based on Antagonism': Ionesco, Pinter, Albee, and Others." In *The Two Faces of Ionesco* edited by Rosette C. Lamont and Melvin J. Friedman, 175–95. Troy, N.Y.: Whitston, 1977.

Fumerton, M. Patricia. "Verbal Prisons: The Language of Albee's *A Delicate Balance*." *English Studies in Canada* 7, no. 2 (1981): 201–11.

Gabbard, Lucina, P. "Albee's *Seascape*: An Adult Fairy Tale." *Modern Drama* 21 (1977): 307–17.

Gabbard, Lucina P. "At the Zoo: From O'Neill to Albee." *Modern Drama* 19 (1975): 365–74.

Gale, Steven H. "Breakers of Illusion: George in Edward Albee's *Who's Afraid of Virginia Woolf?* and Richard in Harold Pinter's *The Lover*." *Vision* 1, no. 1 (1978): 70–77.

Glenn, Jules. "The Adoption Theme in Edward Albee's *Tiny Alice* and *The American Dream*." In *Lives, Events, and Other Players: Directions in Psychobiography*, 255–69. New York: Aronson, 1981.

Goodman, Henry. "The New Dramatists: Edward Albee." *Drama Survey* 2 (1962): 72–79.

Gould, Jean. "Edward Albee and the Current Scene." *Modern American Playwrights*, 273–86. New York: Apollo Editions, 1966.

Green, Charles Lee. *Edward Albee: An Annotated Bibliography 1968–1977.* Studies in Modern Literature 6. New York: AMS.

Gussow, Mel. "Albee: Odd Man In on Broadway." *Newsweek*, 4 February 1963, 49–52.

Hamilton, Kenneth. "Mr. Albee's Dream." *Queen's Quarterly* 70 (1963): 393–99.

Hankiss, Elemer. "Who's Afraid of Edward Albee?" *New Hungarian Quarterly* 5 (1964): 168–74.

Harris, Wendell V. "Morality, Absurdity, and Albee." *Southwest Review* 49 (1964): 249–56.

Hilfer, Anthony Channell. "George and Martha: Sad, Sad, Sad." In *Seven Contemporary Authors*, edited by T. B. Whitbread, 119–40. Austin: University of Texas Press, 1966.

Hirsch, Foster. *Who's Afraid of Edward Albee?* Berkeley: Creative Arts Books Co, 1978.

Kane, Leslie. *The Language of Silence: On the Unspoken and the Unspeakable in Modern Drama.* Madison, N. J.: Fairleigh Dickinson University Press, 1984.

Knepler, Henry. "Conflict of Traditions in Edward Albee." *Modern Drama* 10 (1967): 274–79.

Kostelanetz, Richard. "Edward Albee." *On Contemporary Literature*, 225–31. New York: Avon Books, 1964.

Lewis, Allan. "The Fun and Games of Edward Albee." In *American Plays and Play-wrights of the Contemporary Theatre*, 81–98. New York: Crown, 1965.

Lyons, Charles R. "Two Projections of the Isolation of the Human Soul: Brecht's *Im Dickicht der Staedte* and Albee's *The Zoo Story*." *Drama Survey* 4 (1965): 121–38.

McDonald, Daniel. "Truth and Illusion in *Who's Afraid of Virginia Woolf?*" *Renascence* 17 (1964): 63–69.

Markus, Thomas B. "*Tiny Alice* and Tragic Catharsis." *Educational Theatre Journal* 17 (1965): 225–33.

Mayberry, Robert. "A Theatre of Discord: Some Plays of Beckett, Albee, and Pinter." *Kansas Quarterly* 12, 4 (1979): 7–16.

Miller, Joydan Y. "Myth and the American Dream: O'Neill to Albee." *Modern Drama* (1964): 190–98.

Moses, Robbie Odom. "Death as a Mirror of Life: Edward Albee's *All Over*." *Modern Drama* 19 (1975): 67–77.

Nelson, Gerald. "Edward Albee and His Well-Made Plays." *Tri-Quarterly* 5 (n.d.): 182–88.

Nilan, Mary M. "Albee's *The Zoo Story:* Aliented Man and the Nature of Love." *Modern Drama* 16 (1972): 55–59.

Oberg, Arthur K. "Edward Albee: His Language and Imagination." *Prairie Schooner* 40 (1966): 139–46.

Paolucci, Anne. *From Tension to Tonic: The Plays of Edward Albee*. Carbondale: Southern Illinois University Press, 1971.

Phillips, Elizabeth C. "Albee and the Theatre of the Absurd." *Tennessee Studies in Literature* 10 (1965): 73–80.

Plotinsky, Melvin L. "The Transformations of Understanding: Edward Albee in the Theatre of the Irresolute." *Drama Survey* 4 (Winter 1965): 220–32.

Post, Robert M. "Fear Itself: Edward Albee's *A Delicate Balance*." *CLA Journal* 13 (1969): 163–71.

Roudané, Matthew C. "An Interview with Edward Albee." *Southern Humanities Review* 16 (1982): 29–44.

Roy, Emil. "*Who's Afraid of Virginia Woolf?* and the Tradition." *Bucknell Review* 13 (1965): 27–36.

Rule, Margaret W. "An Edward Albee Bibliography." *Twentieth Century Literature* 14 (1968): 35–44.

Samuels, Charles Thomas. "The Theatre of Edward Albee." *The Massachusetts Review* 6 (1964–65): 187–201.

Schechner, Richard. "Who's Afraid of Edward Albee?" *Tulane Drama Review* 7 (1963): 7–10.

Schneider, Alan. "Why So Afraid?" *Tulane Drama Review* 7 (1963): 10–13.

Valgemae, Mardi. "Albee's Great God Alice." *Modern Drama* 10 (1967): 267–73.

Wallace, Robert S. "*The Zoo Story:* Albee's Attack on Fiction." *Modern Drama* 16 (1972): 49–54.

Wasserman, Julian N., Linsley, Joy L., Kramer, Jerome A., eds. *Edward Albee: An Interview and Essays*. Houston: University of St. Thomas, 1983. [Available from Syracuse University Press].

Witherington, Paul. "Language of Movement in Albee's *The Death of Bessie Smith*." *Twentieth Century Literature* 13 (1967): 84–88.

Wolfe, Peter. "The Social Theatre of Edward Albee." *Prairie Schooner* 39 (1965): 248–62.

Worth, Katherine. "Edward Albee: Playwright of Evolution." In *Essays on Contemporary American Drama* edited by Hedwig Bock and Albert Wertheim. Munich: Hueber, 1981.

Zimbardo, Rose A. "Symbolism and Naturalism in Edward Albee's *The Zoo Story.*" *Twentieth Century Literature* 8 (1962): 10–17.

Acknowledgments

"Albee and the Absurd: *The American Dream* and *The Zoo Story*" by Brian Way from *American Theatre* (Stratford-upon-Avon Studies 10), © 1967 by Edward Arnold (Publishers) Ltd., London. Reprinted by permission.

"Edward Albee: Don't Make Waves" by Gerald Weales from *The Jumping-Off Place: American Drama in the 1960s* by Gerald Weales, © 1969 by Gerald Weales. Reprinted by permission of the author and the Macmillan Company.

"Albee's Gothic: The Resonance of Cliché" by Paul Witherington from *Comparative Drama* (1970), © 1970 by Western Michigan University. Reprinted by permission of the editors of *Comparative Drama*.

"All Over" by Ronald Hayman from *Contemporary Playwrights: Edward Albee* by Ronald Hayman, © 1971 by Ronald Hayman. Reprinted by permission of A.D. Peters & Co. Ltd. and Heinemann Educational Books Ltd.

"Conventional Albee: *Box* and *Chairman Mao*" by Anthony Hopkins from *Modern Drama* 16, no. 2 (September 1973), © 1973 by the University of Toronto, Graduate Centre for the Study of Drama. Reprinted by permission of *Modern Drama*.

"Staging the Unconscious: *Tiny Alice*" by Mary Castiglie Anderson from *Renascence: Essays on Value in Literature* 33 (1979), © 1979 by the Catholic Renascence Society. Reprinted by permission of *Renascence: Essays on Value in Literature* (Marquette University Press).

"The Idea of Language in the Plays of Edward Albee" by Julian N. Wasserman from *Edward Albee: An Interview and Essays*, edited by Julian N. Wasserman, © 1983 by the University of St. Thomas. Reprinted by permission of the University of St. Thomas Press.

"The Limits of Reason: *Seascape* as Psychic Metaphor" by Liam O. Purdon from *Edward Albee: An Interview and Essays*, edited by Julian N. Wasserman, © 1983 by the University of St. Thomas. Reprinted by permission of the University of St. Thomas Press.

"The Pirandello in Albee: *The Lady from Dubuque*" (originally entitled "The Pirandello in Albee: The Problem of Knowing in *The Lady from Dubuque*") by Thomas P.

Adler from *Edward Albee: An Interview and Essays,* edited by Julian N. Wasserman, © 1983 by the University of St. Thomas. Reprinted by permission of the University of St. Thomas Press.

"Who's Afraid of Virginia Woolf?" (originally entitled "Edward Albee") by C. W. E. Bigsby from *A Critical Introduction to Twentieth-Century American Drama, volume 2: Tennessee Williams, Arthur Miller, Edward Albee* by C. W. E. Bigsby, © 1984 by C. W. E. Bigsby. Reprinted by permission of the author and Cambridge University Press.

"The Man Who Had Three Arms" by Matthew C. Roudané from *Understanding Edward Albee* by Matthew C. Roudané, © 1987 by the University of South Carolina Press. Reprinted by permission.

Index